The Present Status and Future Prospects of Reference/Information Service

The Present Status and Future Prospects of Reference/ Information Service

Proceedings of the Conference held at the School of Library Service, Columbia University, March 30—April 1, 1966, under the sponsorship of Columbia University, School of Library Service and American Library Association, Reference Services Division

Edited by
Winifred B. Linderman
Professor of Library Service, Columbia University

American Library Association/*Chicago, 1967*

Library of Congress Catalog Card Number 67-23002

Copyright © 1967 by the American Library Association

Manufactured in the United States of America

Contents

Introduction   *Winifred B. Linderman*   vii

Some Thoughts on the Present Status and Future Prospects
    of Reference Work
                    Keynote address by Verner W. Clapp   1

    Discussion   12

CONSUMERS OF INFORMATION AND LEVELS OF SERVICE

Library Users of Information and Their Needs
                                        Helen M. Focke   21

THE SPECTRUM OF SERVICES OFFERED

A Spacious Closet of Reading   *Marian M. Allen*   34

Reconstruction of Library Services   *Leonard H. Freiser*   48

Broadening the Spectrum   *Alan M. Rees*   57

Comment   *Frances E. Henne*   66

SYSTEMS OF REFERENCE/INFORMATION SERVICE

Regional and State Systems   *John G. Lorenz*   73

The Library Kaleidoscope: National Plans and Planning
                                        Foster E. Mohrhardt   83

    Discussion   93

REFERENCE/INFORMATION SOURCES

Currently Available Tools—Their Adequacy
    for Today's Needs   *Katharine G. Harris*   103

Development of Machine-generated Tools
                                        Pauline A. Atherton   121

Comment   *Edwin B. Colburn*   134

    Discussion   140

INFORMATION STORAGE AND RETRIEVAL SYSTEMS

Development of Storage and Retrieval Systems
                                          Joseph Becker   151

Using Accumulated Knowledge   *Emmanuel G. Mesthene*   157

Comment   *Grieg Aspnes*   165

    Discussion   168

Implications for the Future of Reference/Information Service
                                      Frederick G. Kilgour   172

    Discussion   184

Appendix I. Conference Program   187

Appendix II. Registered Participants   190

Introduction

Winifred B. Linderman

Almost a quarter of a century has elapsed since the Chicago Institute on reference work was held, the proceedings of which were published as *The Reference Function of the Library.* Since that time, as is pointed out in one of these papers, reference service has changed little, although much has happened in the development and acquisition of knowledge, and information has become one of the most important national resources. Recognition of these facts and their implications has brought urgent demands for adaptation to the change and for speedy and efficient means of access to all forms of information.

Confronted with these demands for control and services, libraries, along with other agencies, have looked toward machines for solutions to their problems. As research and experimentation have gone forward, reference librarians, as a group, have tended to remain on the periphery. True, they have accepted machine-produced tools, such as catalogs and bibliographies, and have made increasing use of photocopy, but by and large there seems to have been a reluctance on the part of many to discuss the fundamentals of change, which are demanding new forms and greater depth of service, or the implications for reference service of the developing library networks.

The addition of another institute or conference always gives one pause, but it did seem that the time had come for reference librarians, information specialists, and educators in these fields to meet in a basic, exploratory conference, not only to contemplate the present state of the art, but also to assess future needs and the accompanying problems and to look ahead toward new forms of service and means for coping with demands that must be met if the initiative of supplying information is not to pass to other agencies.

With all this in mind, the Columbia School of Library Service drew up a set of objectives, a tentative program, and a plan of action to discuss with the Board of the Reference Services Division at the Detroit ALA conference. Moral support and agreement to act as cosponsor were immediately forthcoming, and financial support in the form of a grant from the H. W. Wilson Foundation followed shortly. At the request of the Conference Director, Wayne Hartwell, then President of the Reference Services Division, appointed John Fall, Helen M. Focke, and Edward G. Strable as a committee to advise with the Director and Dean Dalton on program and conference plans.

The overall aim of the conference is expressed in the title, but the thinking, the planning, and the hopes went far beyond this. The conference was invitational, limited to about one hundred people selected for their known interests and services in the information/reference field. They represented the various points of view, aspects, and groups identified with this service at all levels, from elementary schools to research organizations. Of prime importance was representation from all parts of the country, because the conference was conceived as a foundation conference from which the participants would go back to their respective sections to set up other conferences which would explore still further the problems, the ideas, and the suggestions brought out at the initial meetings.

Invitations were sent to all library schools accredited at the beginning of 1966, to representative reference librarians in special and public libraries, and to librarians in educational institutions at all levels. A list of alternate people was drawn up, but acceptances from the original list were so complete that only a few on the alternate list could be invited. Scores of interested people who wrote, telephoned, or telegraphed for invitations unfortunately could not be accommodated. Any regional groups planning future conferences will find many persons in all parts of the country anxious to participate.

In line with the conception of the conference, the program was designed to include consideration of the fundamental aspects of reference/information service: the consumers; levels of service; regional, state, subject, and national networks; sources of information; the development of information storage and retrieval systems and the intellectual problems involved; and, finally, the implications for future service of the points brought out at the conference.

The speakers sought were those well known for their conversance with the various topics and for their interest in the information problem. So strong was their belief that this conference was needed, and, in fact, long overdue, that those invited willingly added this assignment to their heavy schedules.

On March 30, 106 persons arrived at Columbia for three days of meetings, during which reference librarians, information specialists, and educators conferred in an effort to discover mutual problems and to consider objectives or goals and various means of achieving them. No plan of action or set of resolutions or specific proposals emerged, largely because this was not the purpose of the conference and none was expected.

The conference sessions were completely tape-recorded. A discussion period followed all but the second session. In the report of the discussions, not everything has been retained, but an attempt has been made to include all questions and comments relevant to the subject of the session and to present them as faithfully as possible. Most of them are given verbatim with only minor editing in the interest of order and brevity. Wherever known, the name of the speaker is given. Where any remarks have been summarized or rephrased to any extent, they are enclosed in parentheses.

Comments at the final session and the expressed hope of the organizers that this basic exploration would lead to state or regional conferences for further study of the problems raised led to the proposal that participants write at once to the conference director, suggesting specific ideas or topics in need of further investigation and recommending procedures for the conduct of future conferences to make them even more productive.

From the seventy letters received, there emerged only two tentative suggestions about procedures—tentative, because each person who mentioned them named the difficulties involved. The first was that papers be prepared and issued in advance, thus allowing more conference time for reaction to them. The second was that speakers remain for the entire conference.

More important were the comments made on the entire conference. In general, those who wrote stated that the meetings had presented a wide and stimulating range of topics; had displayed the new questions and challenges to be met and the complexity and interrelationships of the problems faced; and had drawn attention to the necessity of now relating theory to practice, of developing new practices, and of initiating more research programs. Of the issues mentioned as being in special need of additional exploration, some in future conferences and others in research programs, the following, in one form or another, were suggested more than once:

1. The nature of the reference process and its objectives
2. The way librarians perform reference services
3. The need for greater depth and extension of services
4. The need to take advantage of machines and new techniques if the initiative is not to be lost to outside agencies

5. User characteristics and needs and the way information is used (knowledge necessary if the user is to be part of the system)
6. The impact of the network idea on reference service, or the way the reference librarian will operate within a library network—his intellectual role in a complex of systems
7. The possibility of the reference intermediary being unnecessary
8. Implications of the rapid change in reference/information service on library education—the basic ideas on which teaching programs must be built
9. The question of whether library schools are equipped to carry on the amount and the type of research needed
10. Possibilities inherent in interdisciplinary research.

That the conference succeeded in setting forth the pertinent problems is obvious from the above list, for all of these topics were touched on either directly or by implication, and there was general agreement that all must have further consideration. The interrelationship of these problems was highlighted by bringing together librarians working in diverse programs. The important question now is—what next?

In conclusion the Director wishes to express thanks to many people: the President of the Reference Services Division and the members of the advisory committee whom he appointed; the speakers who took time to prepare papers and to come to the conference; the moderators and commentators who contributed leadership and guidance; and all the participants who attended, and who, whether vocal or not at the conference, wrote to express their ideas, opinions, and reactions and who will surely be assuming further leadership.

Grateful acknowledgment is made to Carlyle Frarey and Mrs. Marilee Martel of the School of Library Service for their help with arrangements and for the assistance of their staff both at the conference and in preparing these proceedings for publication. Special thanks are due Jack Dalton, Dean of the School of Library Service, without whose continuing encouragement, support, and advice the conference would not have been held nor the proceedings published.

Finally, thanks are due particularly to the H. W. Wilson Foundation for recognizing the need for this conference, and by their financial support making it possible.

September 30, 1966   *Winifred B. Linderman*

Some Thoughts on the Present Status and Future Prospects of Reference Work

Keynote address by Verner W. Clapp

Reference work, as we who have labored in its vineyard have always maintained, is the culmination, the flowering—or, if you will, the reaping and the reward—of library work. For this, from generation to generation, the acquisitions staff has checked dealers' catalogs, bid at auctions, ransacked the bookshops and bookstalls of the world, engaged in inequitable exchanges, and sought out tons of unreadable official publications. For this the bibliophiles collected, and then parted with, their collections again. For this the never ceasing labors of the cataloging room slowly wrought streamlined order out of incredible chaos, converting an inapprehensible miscellaneity into a comprehensible universe of knowledge. For this the army of encyclopedists, lexicographers, compilers, bibliographers, and indexers selected and anthologized, analyzed and assembled, footnoted and referenced. Of all these labors this, at last, is the payoff. The time may seem to be any time of day. But it is not just any time of day; it is the very moment of truth. In this instant, out of the secret lore, the powerful wisdom that has been entrusted to him, the reference librarian has pronounced an Open Sesame, and the recesses of the library unfold. From among its thousands of volumes and millions of pages shines forth a fact— the information for which an inquirer is waiting at the reference desk, perhaps patiently, perhaps impatiently, and only rarely conscious of the miracle that is being performed on his behalf and which is taking place before his eyes.

Verner W. Clapp, President of the Council on Library Resources, Incorporated, was formerly chief assistant librarian of the Library of Congress. He is author of *The Future of the Research Library*, the Windsor lectures for 1963.

There is a wonderful story in the *Arabian Nights* of the goings-
on one evening in Baghdad. It all started when a tailor and his wife
picked up a hunchback, who turned out to be the Sultan's jester, and
took him home for conversing and carousing. During the evening,
the hunchback choked to death on a bone. Reluctant to be caught
with a corpse on their hands, the couple carried it to the home of a
physician and left it in a dark hallway. A whole series of events
follows until finally the body is returned to the Sultan, the whole
story comes out, and the Sultan says, "Let this story be written in
letters of gold around the audience chamber!"

And so it should be with this word, this text, this piece of information which the reference librarian has charmed out of the
collections of the library. It should be inscribed in letters of gold
around the reference room. The inquirer, the beneficiary, does
not appreciate the magic of what he has seen; he thinks the text is
mere black and white, but it is a golden legend.

When I was a member of the public reference staff of a large
library some years ago, we were a kind of elite, very conscious of
our opportunities and our abilities. We knew that we were the real
possessors of the key. Better than others, we could run rings
around the catalog—exploit its resources while compensating for
its deficiencies. We were intimate—as were also only those who
maintained them—with the special records and files. We were
familiar not only with the reference and classified collections, but
with uncataloged deposits and arrears of which few other persons
seemed to be conscious. We could tap the resources of other divisions and departments, including the special knowledge of members
of their staffs. We could conduct forced-draft searches of the
Congressional Record by five footcandles of light, and we often
climbed ten full stack levels on the run when hydraulic elevators
failed. And we always—well, nearly always—produced our fact. It
was an article of faith with us that somewhere in print in the library
was the answer to every question, and that we—sometimes only we—
could produce it. I find myself still believing this.

Withal, we recognized that it was not personal merit but special opportunity that endowed us with these capabilities. We were
very conscious of the responsibilities entailed, and we were very
conscious of the rewards.

The rewards, besides the immediate one of satisfying an inquirer or an inquiry, were of two kinds. The first was that we were
able to participate in searches of the most exhilarating kind, because to us came questions that were, by definition, important to
the questioners, and for which other information systems had often
failed to produce the answers. The second was that, again and
again, we were able to bring to the answer of such a question a

book of which no use might have been expected in a hundred years, if ever. As long as I served as a member of that reference staff, I never lacked for stories. My days were filled with exciting searches ending in fascinating books. What reference librarian would not relish having participated in bringing to the dating of a Shakespearean sonnet a contemporary engineer's account of the erection of the obelisk in St. Peter's Square?

Reference service, as I have described it, seems so simple, so natural, and so necessary. But we all know that no matter how desirable, it does not always come that simply or naturally.

Why, in the first place, is reference service, in the sense of a special staff, necessary? Why can't the collection service itself? A partial answer to this question is, of course, that a reference staff is required to take care of telephone calls and inquiries by mail. This being granted, why is a reference staff required to take care of inquiries from readers in person?

There is something of a paradox here. A library is, by definition, composed of units, each of which is a package of information. Now the packaging of these units, their format, as distinct from their contents which differ from package to package, embodies the results of several thousands of years of experimentation in providing convenient storage of recorded information and access to it. I am referring to the physical makeup, the title page which announces the contents, the table of contents which further provides a guide to them, the chapter headings, and so on—all the bibliographical apparatus, ending up with a bibliography, appendixes, index, etc. Now, in order to facilitate access to these records and to further their usefulness, the library has imposed upon them, in addition, its own form of bibliographic organization, again making use of techniques developed over hundreds, if not thousands, of years. A principal element in this technique of organization is the catalog, a device with the capacity for organizing enormous quantities of facts and for greatly facilitating the retrieval of information about potential sources of information.

Why, may it be asked, does a device (the catalog), possessing such capacity and versatility, a device that aims and claims to be able to lead to information throughout the library—why does it fail so conspicuously in providing information regarding itself? Why must it be complemented by a staff of human assistants, possessing much less accurate and much shorter memories than its own?

We all know some of the answers to this question, but I doubt if anyone has supplied a complete answer. And I think that a complete answer might greatly improve our understanding of the function of the catalog and the nature of the reference process.

The use of the catalog in reference work has been much discussed, and the presence of each element of information on the

catalog card has been loudly defended as having been useful at one
time or another for answering reference questions. But I do not
recall a discussion of the extent to which the reference work load
might be increased or decreased by varying the informational content of the catalog, or of what would be required of the catalog to
reduce the reference load still further, perhaps to zero, and what
the cost might be.

Yet there are a number of interesting topics implicit in such a
discussion, and a number of interesting questions might be asked.
What kinds of information, for example, are sought by inquirers
from libraries but are not readily reached by them through the
catalog? Is there something in the nature of the beast that makes
this so, or can the catalog be changed? Is it desirable that it
should be changed? Do conditions in this connection vary with the
subject interest involved?

There is no doubt, for example, that much of the work of the
reference staff consists in giving instruction in the use of library
tools and procedures. It appears to follow that adequate prior instruction would significantly free the reference staff for other work.
But how to effect such prior instruction? This is a problem of long
standing in colleges and universities, where no universally satisfactory solution has been found. One of the best contributions to a
solution is, of course, adequate instruction at secondary-school
level. Although this is probably increasing, the problem may be
expected to endure and even to magnify, with the prospect that, for a
long period, time will be taken from reference staffs that could be
put to better use. Programmed teaching machines at appropriate
points in the library offer an alternative solution which has not
been sufficiently tried. Is this something that should be of interest
to the reference service?

Along the same line, I have always been bothered that Winchell
and similar works (Malclès, Walford, Besterman, *Index Bibliogra-
phicus,* etc.) seem to be the peculiar property of the reference desk
and its staff. But, surely, some of these (perhaps just the first) are
books with which every schoolboy, certainly every graduate student
and every faculty member, should be conversant. These are not
the reference books of various disciplines, but of library work itself. They are so general that nobody ever teaches their use to
anyone except librarians, and I am afraid that librarians often keep
them behind the desk, just to be sure that they are always there. If
the use of these books is not discovered in secondary school, where
is it to be learned, and how is it to be taught? If not at the reference desk, then perhaps, again, by a teaching machine.

Some years ago, with a view to ascertaining just what reference service consists of, it was proposed in a large New England

university library to tape-record the dialogues between reference
staff and inquirers. Although the project offered difficulties, and
so far as I know was never executed, it might still be conducted
with profit. If information of this kind could be assembled from a
number of institutions of various kinds, it might become possible
to identify the factors that distinguish one library public from
another and that dictate the kind of reference service needed by
each public.

What is the relation between reference books and reference
work? We learn, on the one hand, that in one large public library,
less than a third of the reference questions are answered by reference books. Try, on the other hand, to imagine the task of a reference staff working with Dr. Spofford's recommended collection of
reference books, which is described in the U.S. Office of Education's 1876 *Survey of Public Libraries in the United States*.[1] In
this collection of 650 titles, although it included a reference book
on life after death, many of the sources of information (such as the
Statistical Abstract, Granger, or *Pauly-Wissowa*) which a present-
day staff takes for granted, and without which it would spend many
hours running down scattered information, were, of course, not yet
represented. The fact is that each good reference book as it appears adds significantly to the reference staff's efficiency. If this
is so, then the efficiency of the staff has been very greatly increased since 1876. What has happened to the time and money
saved? Have they gone into more and better reference work, or
into a reduction of staff size in proportion to inquirers served?
This would be an interesting question to investigate, and the answers might have interesting implications. Would it, for example,
be possible to plan reference books as part of a program for
making most efficient use of reference staffs?

I am not trying to put the reference staff out of business, but I
am trying to do for them what was done for me. When I was young
and we got into the nice, warm summer months, our public left.
Then the reference staff found time for its own pursuits, and we
could hardly wait for those boiling summer months to come so that
we could get down to our own work. This was the time when we
learned to use our library.

While the reference services of public and academic libraries
have continued to follow traditional lines and to be rendered to
their traditional publics, there have grown up in the past twenty

_____

[1] Ainsworth R. Spofford, "Works of Reference for Libraries," in U.S. Bureau of Education, *Public Libraries in the United States of America, Their
History, Condition, and Management* (Dept. of the Interior, Bureau of Education, Special Report, Part I [Washington, D.C.: Govt. Print. Off., 1876; 2v. in
1]), p.686-710.

years new forms of public reference service which at first served
as exceptions to usual practice, but which, from their multiplication
and acceptance, now appear to be establishing the rule. Although
one should perhaps be hesitant in describing as a revolution a development that is taking place as gradually as this, it must be said
that the development gives prospect of effecting a genuine revolution in the sense of altering our traditions.

   This revolution was long delayed. It commenced before World
War I and was halted by that conflict; it was once again set into
motion by World War II and its subsequent events.

   Before World War I, the scientific world had girded itself,
under the leadership of the Royal Society of London, to engage in
cooperative international action to control the science information
explosion of that day. As a result, it had launched the *International
Catalogue of Scientific Literature* which commenced coverage with
the year 1901 and ended in 1914 after 238 volumes. When the *Catalogue* failed to give bibliographic control as hoped, the energy involved in its production would undoubtedly have been diverted into
more useful channels if World War I had not, in terminating the
enterprise, also damaged the basis for further cooperative action.
So numbed and disillusioned with respect to bibliographical projects was the scientific world by the failure that it did little more
about the problem until after World War II. In fact, even when the
American Library Association, in the United States in the thirties,
attempted to organize joint action with scientists and engineers on
the major bibliographic problems of their fields, it encountered
apathy.

   World War II, however, and even more the events of the subsequent Cold War, called the attention of scientists once more, and
that of many engineers for the first time, to the need for improving
access to the literature of and information in their subjects. The
effects of these events were reinforced by a development of a totally different kind. This was the development of the unpublished
scientific-technical research report, which came into its own
during the war as the result of the need for separate publication
and security classification of documents. That was the need; the
actual production was greatly facilitated by the perfection at just
about that time of office duplicating machines, especially of the
photo-offset sort.

   From these origins have come developments typically in either
of two forms. One is the establishment of a center or series of
centers to facilitate access to the reports and other documents resulting from research and development performed on behalf of one
or more federal agencies; these arrangements have their anteced-
ents in the depository system for government documents. The
other is the establishment of a center for extracting, assembling,

and servicing information (as contrasted with documents) in a specialized field of science or engineering. Thus in the United States
there are, on the one hand, depository centers for patents and for
the reports related to atomic energy and space; on the other hand,
there are centers for information about defense metals, thermo-
physical properties, infrared spectra, the characteristics of chem-
icals in cancer therapy, etc. There is even a referral center from
which an inquirer may learn of other sources of information. Access
to the services of these centers is not always on the same level; in
some cases, it is available only to government contractors; in others,
it is available to industrial concerns on a fee basis; in others, still
other qualifications or arrangements are involved.

The fact is, however, that the contemporary industrial research
scientist or engineer, who may already be served by his company's
special library or, in some cases, by the special services to industry provided by a few university, research, and public libraries, is
rapidly becoming accustomed to draw upon a national reference
network, which he consults for the most part through an intermediary, receiving its results either in the form of lists of citations
or abstracts or "hard copy" or informative statements. There are
indications, as might be anticipated, that the expectation of such
service is extending to the members of scientific and engineering
faculties.

Meanwhile, too, the responsibilities of government with respect
to the provision of scientific, technical, and other information for
use in business, industry, research, education, and medicine have
become common subjects of discussion and investigation at the top-
most levels of government: in Congressional committees and in
the Executive offices. Out of these discussions and investigations,
there emerge from time to time plans for national informational
services. Although these plans at first may show insufficient com-
prehension of the mechanisms which they discuss or in other ways
fall short of their targets, yet it may be expected that sooner or
later the tendencies and pressures which they represent will gradually force the development of reference services which are much
more "complete" (I am using that word in the Rothstein "complete"
versus "conservative" antinomy) and much less "conservative"
than the traditional services. Between now and then, however, the
individual library will have to discover whether its conservative
service can be transmuted into a complete service, even with the
aid of national centers. Perhaps some suggestions for such a
transmutation may be heard during the present conference.

But, of course, the self-sufficiency of the local reference service will not be affected only by the existence of national reference
centers. Already there is writing on the wall. (It is actually the
trace of a light-pen on the face of a cathode-ray tube.) What the

writing says is, "You are now on-line to the national reference system."

Actually, this will be only an extension of what we are doing today. Any reference librarian who makes a telephone call in the course of his search, whether to another department of the library or in town or by long distance, is to that extent going on-line into the national reference system. Already, too, we have examples of regional coordination of reference work: sometimes through centralization in the most competent library of a group; sometimes in a reverse-flow cascade by which a question is referred successively upward until it reaches the level at which it can be effectively answered; sometimes in a decentralized plan in which it is dealt with by the best qualified, for that particular question, of a number of libraries. Meanwhile, waiting in the wings are other plans whose grand ambition it is to put the entire library resources of a region to use for the benefit of the entire population of that region. From these, it is but a step to a national reference service system such as is being discussed this weekend at the annual conference of the Reference, Special, and Information Section of the (British) Library Association at Cardiff.

It should be noted that the advent of such a system is not delayed for want of technological support. Technological support, in fact, is quite sufficient: the telephone, teletype, photoduplication, telefacsimile (scarcely needed as yet), and postal and delivery service. The item in which there is deficiency is human labor. Conducting reference work requires a human being capable of looking into the catalog and consulting the collections. No library can be expected, without compensation, to divert a significant part of its reference capability to the service of inquirers in other libraries. There are two ways to overcome this obstacle. The first is to compensate libraries for the required diversion of manpower; the second is to mechanize or automate reference work to make diversion of manpower unnecessary.

The first of these is the method hitherto used for the development of regional reference arrangements. Here, a government body actually subsidizes services from a library capable of extending its services to the libraries of a group; in some way or other, it arranges for an allocation of compensation by which each library is rewarded corresponding to its service.

As for the second method, at first glance one might be inclined to say that there are no examples. Actually, however, some important prototypes exist. In the case of the National Library of Medicine, for example, automation plays an important role in the production of the *Index Medicus*. This is a publication which not only is the principal record of the current journal literature of medicine, but also can be used as a record of the library's holdings

of this literature. Items listed in the *Index* may be confidently requested from the library, if not available closer at hand.

Now the promptness of publication of the *Index,* which is made
possible by automation in the first place, has the effect of giving
inquirers at a distance a facility of access to the library's collections substantially equal to that of inquirers on its premises. But
there is more to the prototype than just this. As is generally
known, the *Index* reproduces, but does not exhaust, the information
recorded on the computer (MEDLARS) tapes. Consequently, to
serve those who wish to make exhaustive searches, the library deposits copies of the tapes at various centers, where they may be
used either for literature searches or as the basis of a notification
service or for still other reference services—all equally as well
as though they were conducted in the National Library of Medicine
itself. The January *Bulletin* of the Medical Library Association
carried an account of the use of the MEDLARS tapes at the Colorado
Medical Center.[2]

Thus, automation has made it possible to extend the reference
facilities of a great library without diversion of its own reference
manpower. It is true, however, that when inquirers wish to see
journal articles for which they found references in the *Index
Medicus* but which are not available to them locally their requests
add to the library's work load over and above that which is created
by inquirers on the premises.

In this respect, the prototype of a mechanized reference system established by the National Aeronautics and Space Administration goes one step further. Like the National Library of Medicine,
it has a periodically published bibliography which is also the catalog of a collection; like it, there are regional service centers where
computer tapes are available for intensive searches and can also
serve as a basis for announcement services. In addition, to the
extent that the indexed material consists of noncopyright research
reports, copies may be procured from a locally available depository set of microfiches. Thus the two conditions are fulfilled:
searches can be made in the catalog and use can be made of the
collections, all without diversion of reference manpower of the
central agency.

These are examples of admittedly "off-line" applications of
computers and other devices to reference work. Other examples,
such as the computer-derived concordance and the KWIC index,
will, I presume, be discussed later in this conference. That these
have already made a significant contribution to reference work
cannot be doubted. Neither, by the same token, can it be doubted

_____
[2] Frank B. Rogers, "MEDLARS Operating Experience at the University of
Colorado," *Bulletin of the Medical Library Association,* 54:1-10 (Jan., 1966).

that the on-line applications, which will assuredly follow in due
course and which are the subject of the INTREX inquiry at Massachusetts Institute of Technology, will possess an even greater sig-
nificance. We shall be hearing about the work that is being done on
them from some of those who are actually involved in the effort to
bring them about.

In 1876, Ainsworth Rand Spofford said, in the course of introducing his suggestions for a reference collection, "Public libraries
are useful to readers in proportion to the extent and ready supply
of the helps they furnish to facilitate researches of every kind.
... That is the best library and he the most useful librarian by
whose aid every reader is enabled to put his finger on the fact he
wants just when it is wanted."[3]

"Them's fine words," as the man said. They have the additional merit of being as true today as when they were first uttered.
If they now seem inadequate, that is not because we have been able
to comply completely with their monitions and progressed to a
higher plateau of doctrine. Rather, we have come to recognize that
the doctrine, as framed by Dr. Spofford and his successors, down to
very recent decades was, in effect, without intending to be so, a
doctrine of passivity, and we have matched it with a doctrine of
initiative. For the formulation of the latter, we are indebted to
special library work. There, where the library is typically an or-
ganic member of a corporate enterprise, it is natural that it should
take the initiative in supplying information rather than wait to be
asked. Hence the motto, "Putting information to work"; hence current notification services, "selective dissemination of information,"
circularization of periodicals, etc. Although "complete" reference
service is not the same as "dynamic," or "conservative" the same
as "passive," there is likely to be a certain amount of correspondence.

It is interesting to note the differences in acceptance of these
doctrines. The active principal has found its acceptance, as suggested, chiefly in the libraries of industrial and commercial concerns, where information has a money value and where there is a
no-nonsense attitude with respect to the virtue which may accrue
to an inquirer by his digging out the information for himself. With
the techniques available until recently, academic libraries, by contrast, though equally integral members of a corporate body, have
been unable to afford to accept the doctrine of dynamism because of
the sheer number and diversity of interests which they serve. (In
academe it is, moreover, still esteemed virtuous to dig out the information for yourself, and having someone do it for you seems to
require a certain amount of justification.) Still another picture is
presented by legislative reference services. These were born with

---

[3]Ainsworth R. Spofford, *op. cit.*, p.686.

the spoon of initiative in their mouths, their tasks being typically to assemble, digest, and disseminate information bearing on issues likely to receive legislative attention. Finally, one would suppose that the conditions for an active library reference service might most readily be found in a government bureau. Here one might expect to find the common objective which the library shares with other parts of the organization. Typically, however, the service of such libraries is too often found to be passive rather than active, conservative rather than complete; and a number of cases could be cited where the efforts of government librarians to develop a dynamic service have been discouraged or even reversed.

That part of the public which has benefited from a dynamic library service is very small indeed; and even this portion tends, I think, to regard such a service as a condition and benefit of employment, rather than as something applicable to other affairs of life. Even that portion of the public which has made any use of reference services is still very small. The fact is that the public generally is unaware of the existence of such service, is not conditioned to seek it, and is untrained in expressing its needs for information in terms which might be met by such service. As a result, commercial information services, which, without saying so, frequently depend upon libraries for their results, flourish.

I shall not soon forget Marian Carnovsky's story of entertaining Dr. Ranganathan at dinner. Mrs. Carnovsky, herself a librarian, and anxious to avoid dietary embarrassment in entertaining the distinguished Indian library leader, had sought information with respect to an appropriate menu from the hostess service of the *Chicago Tribune*. The information was forthcoming, but Mrs. Carnovsky was annoyed at herself when it was accidentally revealed that the information was furnished by the Chicago Public Library. If even librarians fail to turn instinctively to libraries for information, it is hardly a matter for surprise if others also fail to do so.

But this anecdote, if it does anything at all, merely explodes the better-mousetrap theory. Nobody ever beat his way through a forest to find the maker of better mousetraps. Rather, the maker was "discovered" in the most conspicuous place in the bazaar, surrounded by barkers all shouting "This way to the better mousetrap!" And so it is with reference services. The Chicago Public Library will do the work and the *Tribune* will get the credit so long as the one shouts its wares but the other does not.

At any one moment, one can see only a very short distance into the future. Of the future of reference service, we can only say with certainty at this point that there is excitement in store for it when it at length goes on-line to the national reference system.

Discussion

Ciolli: I would like to refer to the early part of Mr. Clapp's talk, in which he speaks of freeing the reference librarian for other work. Could you give us an example or two?

Clapp: I spoke of the summer months when our public left and we used the time released in compiling bibliographies and in getting to know the collections. I used to disappear from the reference desk every day at 2 P.M. and did not come back until 4:30 P.M. I had two and a half hours to wander around the collections, and what I did was under my own control. I discovered more good books then than I shall ever have a chance to read. I made long lists. There were other discoveries, like missing pages and plates and books that needed binding, and all the things one finds when he really gets to look at the books in a way that so many of us never have a chance to do any more.

Question: I would like to ask Mr. Clapp if his keynote isn't summarized in his recent article in the *Library Journal*[1] about the paper problem, and then I have two questions: (1) Didn't you check the New York Public Library for this book? and (2) Do you have great hopes that the new developments we are to discuss will at least lower the percentage of this kind of mishap?

Clapp: The reference is to an article that I wrote citing a work by John Murray, *Practical Remarks on Modern Paper,* which I said was very scarce. The *National Union Catalog* listed only one copy in the United States—at Princeton—besides the one in the Library of Congress. This is a fact for which I can vouch— that is all the *National Union Catalog* did list. Since then I have

---

[1]Verner W. Clapp, "Closing the Circuit: Automation and Data Processing for Libraries," *Library Journal,* 91:1165-71 (Mar. 1, 1966).

noted two other copies in the country. One is at the New York
Public Library, and this, of course, should have been listed in
the *National Union Catalog*. The other one is at the University
of Vermont in Burlington. I received notice about this one from
the librarian, who says it is part of a large collection on papermaking there, but I wonder if its contents are listed in the
National Union Catalog. I wrote back to ask him but haven't
heard. Apparently there are some very interesting and important books in the collection.

    Now you asked a second question. Do I think that the de-
velopments in this conference or elsewhere may contribute to
removing the obstacles to the dissemination of information
(that is what I was identifying in the *Library Journal* article)
which have withheld the Murray observations on paper from
the mainstream of paper research for a century?

    First, if I am sure of anything, it is that our techniques
for maintaining union catalogs are obsolete. This is not my
conclusion; this is the conclusion of anybody who has ever had
anything to do with a ten-million-card catalog. The card technique is no longer valid—we must find another technique. I am
very hopeful indeed that we can get a new technique, not necessarily the computer in any of its present forms, to improve our
knowledge of the existence and location and availability of books
and, if I may say so, of the kind of information they are capable
of giving. Because, let me remind you, no matter how many
copies of John Murray's book are listed in the union catalog
(there were only two there when there should have been four
that we know of), it would not have done anybody any good unless he had known that there was a book about papermaking by
John Murray. That information is not to be found in either of
the bibliographies on deterioration of paper. Consequently, we
need a better technique for providing this kind of information.

    Second, reference work in the future, I foresee, will make
much greater use of the enormous bibliographical store available than it has in the past. At the moment, it does not do the
reference librarian in the U.S. Department of Agriculture any
good to know that there is a *National Union Catalog* up the
street, because he cannot turn to it. At the moment, the *National Union Catalog* is really for the person who can make a
personal visit. Any other kind of consultation is difficult and
inconvenient, slow and expensive. On-line consultations, if we
can develop them, and I think we can, may still be somewhat
expensive, but at least we will get rid of the other obstacles to
use—delay and inconvenience.

Question: (In view of two points you made—that the number of people

who ever use libraries is relatively small and that increasingly
automated service will demand the assistance of an intermediary reference librarian—are there drastic changes which we
should begin to make, especially in academic libraries, in
methods of instruction on the use of reference tools?)

Clapp: I agree that it is true that only a few people now realize or
are excited by the quantities of interesting information available in books in libraries and are willing to go to the trouble
of searching it out. I think, however, that as people become
more and more used to libraries, acclimated to their use, and
interested and excited by their contents, this group will enlarge.
Instructing people in the use of libraries is part of the business.
It is not enough to give people interesting books to read from
time to time. We have to show them that in libraries these
books are organized into useful and comprehensible organisms.
The time for instruction in this cannot start too early. It should
really start in primary school and should continue throughout
secondary school, where there are innumerable possibilities.

I am sure, however, that there is very little use in taking
an hour of a college freshman's life to make him look at a
motion picture entitled "This Is Your Library." There is little
more use in taking him on a conducted tour or sending people
around with slides, and so on. The principal reason is that
this comes at a time of the student's life when his mind is preoccupied with an enormous number of more interesting matters—matters which are of greater immediate impact. No, the
time to tell people about work in libraries is when they need it.
Of course, they cannot come and ask for an illustrated lecture,
because the illustrated lecture is much too costly to put on for
one person who happens to want at this moment to look up some
references to periodical articles. It would seem to me that
this is an ideal situation for teaching machines. Ideal! And
here we are—in the what year of teaching machines? Does
anyone know of any attempt to use them?

Jenkins: One of our doctoral candidates is making a study of the
use of teaching machines, comparing the rate of learning by
use of the machine and by the classroom approach.

Clapp: Actually, at Mount San Antonio College in California, a
teaching program has been developed and put on two machines,
one at the public catalog and one at the periodical index desk.
However, in this case, it is the machine that is unsatisfactory.
It is one of those machines where the user has to return or
restore the program to zero, or something like that, when he
gets through. The students had not learned to do this and left
it in disorder, which annihilated it for use by the next person.

The college hopes to go on with this program, but it seems to me we are moving very slowly in this field.

Dalton: While you are thinking of the next question, I would like to call attention to the report of the Citizens Committee on Communications which was made to The White House Conference on International Cooperation in December. I think the report has a bearing on this topic in that it provides a new extension to the kind of reference services we are talking about. As some of you know, this committee is not composed of people who are just dreaming about things. It is composed of the President and Chairman of the Board of the International Telephone and Telegraph Corporation; the President of American Broadcasting Corporations, Inc.; the Chairman of the Board of the American Telephone and Telegraph Company; the Chairman of the Board of Radio Corporation of America; and the Editor of the Denver Post. I quote the recommendation it made to the President:

> ...It is recommended that the United States propose and support the establishment by the United Nations of an agency to act as a world source of knowledge and reference for the collection, communication, and dissemination of all types of information useful for peaceful purposes throughout the world. It is recommended that this agency should be called the VOICE OF PEACE.
>
> The VOICE OF PEACE could be established and staffed on a continuous basis by the developed nations of the world. It would constitute a central point of information, query, storage, and reference for use by all participating nations. The computer based center would gather, store, process, program, retrieve, and distribute information and advice on the broadest possible scale. Where requested information is unavailable or where the stored information needs to be supplemented, queries will be referred to experts. Among these experts we would expect that there would be programmers to handle the minimal computer programming effort required. The staff should comprise qualified professionals in various fields, such as medicine, agriculture, meteorology, and all of the other numerous areas in which expertise is important. The staff could be established on a rotating basis with specified periods of service, and presumably, a small cadre of permanent employees.

Now get this:

The functioning of the VOICE OF PEACE would require and should be based upon the establishment of a
world-wide system of communication largely through
presently existing international facilities and enterprises.
There are sufficient telecommunications systems now
available to handle the anticipated VOICE OF PEACE
traffic in the immediate future.[2]

Clapp: I have never seen this; I would like to know more about it.
Has anything happened since?

Dalton: No, I don't think any action has been taken on *any* of the
recommendations made at the White House Conference, but
those of you who were there know that there have been reactions from all sorts of people who are beginning to move. I
think the point that interested me most about this was that
people like Keppel and some of the others just say flatly that
we now have the systems we need to go into operation on a
worldwide basis. And they recommended that the President
and others like the President support this.

Clapp: Few things that we could do could be more important, if not
in themselves, at least in their implications—the implications
of one world of information and, even more important, the
means of securing it. For example, it has always bothered me
that the federal libraries of Washington, built up at enormous
public expense, are still not easily available to the ordinary
member of the American public for the kind of services which
they are capable of giving, namely, access to any informational
record in the world. This facility, it seems to me, should be
made available to every taxpayer and would require only a very
simple organization superimposed on what already exists to
make it so. But by the same token, if this facility is available
for the American taxpayer, doesn't it become available to the
non-American taxpayer?

I have been in foreign countries where I have talked to
people who have written to Washington, only to have their requests vanish as in a bottomless pit. This is perhaps because
they did not know exactly where to write, or perhaps because
the recipient agency did not quite know how to handle the request. This proposal intends to make it possible for the inquiries to get through and get some kind of response. The

[2]National Citizens' Commission on International Cooperation, Committee
on Communications, *Report of the Committee on Communications;* prepared
for presentation at The White House Conference on International Cooperation,
Nov. 28-Dec. 1, 1965 (Doc/14, Final draft. Washington, D.C.: Govt. Print.
Off., 1965, 0-793-675), p.20-21.

important thing, in my estimation, is to train the members of
the public to look for information. But they cannot be trained
to look for information unless it is given to them on those few
occasions when they do look.

(A Visitor from Athens: If money were to be allocated for a
project like the VOICE OF PEACE, should it not be given to
the library association in each country rather than to a new
organization?)

Dalton: I cannot speak for any other country, but I know that library associations in this country are not prepared either to
carry on such work or, if they were given all the money that
would be required, to organize and support and produce the effort that is being asked for here. And I suspect that would be
true of most library associations of the world. At the level at
which these gentlemen are proposing it, it goes beyond our
competence. Does anyone disagree?

Clapp: Mr. Chairman, the techniques which are being proposed
here are really, for the most part, of fairly recent perfection.
Things like Telstar have not been with us very long; telefacsimile methods have only very limited use as yet; the long-
distance telephone has become reasonable in cost in this country only within the last decade or so; and computers have not
really as yet been put to reference work. Now, however, we
are coming into an era in which there are fantastic technological possibilities. Librarians are not the only ones who are
conscious of these, and already there is very great competition
as to who will use them.

Let me remind you of the organization now called EDUCOM.
This is the Interuniversity Communications Council begun at
the University of Michigan with a grant of $750,000 from the
Kellogg Foundation to promote among universities communication having a computer basis. The Council does not know what
it is going to do; it is looking for a program. Dr. Miller of the
University of Michigan, who is a leading spirit, is touring the
country and holding meetings here and there. This month he
is holding a very large meeting at Duke University, where the
whole range of possibilities of computer-based or on-line
communications between university campuses will be discussed.[3]

And so it is elsewhere. Some of you know about the proposal for a national science and technology information network

---

[3] For a statement on EDUCOM, including the objectives, see U.S. Library
of Congress, *Information Bulletin*, 25:434-35 (July 21, 1966—Appendix III, Report of the ARL meeting, July 9, 1966).

launched for discussion by the Office of Science and Technology
in the Executive offices of the President, based on a study made
for the Office by the System Development Corporation of California. Here, again, there is a proposal for a national network
for information purposes, in this case scientific and technical
information. It brings libraries in as one of the factors, but
one of the least important factors, because it is presumed that
libraries are much more interested in the out-of-date, obsolete
information with which their shelves are cluttered than in the
bright and shiny new information which NASA and AEC work on.

To conclude a long harangue, the answer to the question is
that the members of the Committee on Communications work
from their experience, which consists of commercial, industrial, and engineering communications. If we librarians have
a vision of what might be accomplished, using the library as
the base, we had better get in quick and demonstrate the possibilities and sell the story to industrial- and engineering-
minded compatriots.

Consumers of Information and Levels of Service

Library Users of Information and Their Needs
                              Helen M. Focke   21

The Spectrum of Services Offered

A Spacious Closet of Reading   *Marian M. Allen*   34

Reconstruction of Library Services
                              Leonard H. Freiser   48

Broadening the Spectrum   *Alan M. Rees*   57

Comment   *Frances E. Henne*   66

Library Users of Information and Their Needs

Helen M. Focke

My assignment to discuss library users and their needs for reference and information service "at all levels and in all types of service areas" is a rather big one and also has a "cradle-to-the-grave" sound about it. Such a discussion could present a truly overwhelming task if it were carried out completely. To be thorough, it should be backed up by pages of impressive statistics, objectively compiled, with many footnotes, charts, and appendixes, and with questions posed and answered in an orderly and well-substantiated fashion. This paper will not fulfill such requirements. Statistics and precise data will not be presented, because conclusive ones do not seem to exist. Many questions will be posed, but few, if any, will be answered.

Nor is it my intention to present here a detailed literature survey. There have been several recent "state of the art" papers on reference services and useful bibliographic compilations which have done this very well, and it is not necessary to attempt another. Two of the latest are the series of papers in the special reference issue of *Library Trends* for January, 1964,[1] and, even more recently, the current issue on "Library Service to Industry."[2] With these, the *Bibliography of Use Studies*, by Davis and Bailey,[3] a

---

Helen M. Focke, Professor, School of Library Science, Western Reserve University, has served as president of the ALA Reference Services Division and as chairman of the Subscription Books Committee. She is author of the section on pure and applied sciences in Shores' *Basic Reference Sources*.

▶ [1] "Current Trends in Reference Services," *Library Trends*, v.12, no. 3 (Jan., 1964).

[2] "Library Service to Industry," *Library Trends*, v.14, no. 3 (Jan., 1966).

[3] Richard A. Davis and C. A. Bailey, *Bibliography of Use Studies*; prepared for Office of Science Information Service, National Science Foundation,

21

check of *Library Literature, Public Library Abstracts,* and a few
other recent sources, a good outline of what we know and of what
we think we know about reference and information services in
libraries can be obtained. I would rather point out some of the
things which we do not know about users and their needs, perhaps
question some of the assumptions we have made, and suggest
directions for further study.

One way to begin a survey of users of information might be to
think of the child at the "Why, Daddy?" stage, who, at a very early
age, is doing just what the advanced research workers in many of
our recent "use studies" have been shown to do. He has asked
someone who knows or who he fully believes can give him the answer. At the prereading level, the demand for information by the
child may, if the parent does anything beside giving the most obvious answer, drive the conscientious father to seek the answer
occasionally in a nearby library. (Of course, we know, as I recently
saw it expressed in some newspaper Sunday supplement, that "there
are questions no man can answer, and most of them are known to
five-year-olds.")

When the child has learned to read, the "why" questions and
the "what, where, when, and how" questions may result—in a book-
oriented family, at least—in the suggestion that he look them up in
the home encyclopedia or a schoolbook; or he may be told to ask
his teacher, who in turn may refer him to a library. My own memories of the "look-it-up-yourself" response tie in closely with our
family's proud acquisition of the old *Century Dictionary* and a
collection of little pamphlets on birds, trees, snakes, stars, and
mushrooms, while my brothers' questions were often answered by
the *American Boys' Handybook* and *Popular Mechanics.* If a library
had been nearby, instead of four miles away, we surely would have
been urged to use it for information, but it was not until I was
twelve that I was allowed to take the long streetcar ride to the Main
Cleveland Public Library, where opportunities to satisfy my curi-
osity were greatly multiplied. I must confess, however, that I
seldom asked a librarian for help, because I (like many of our adult
patrons, I suspect) was not sure just how to ask for what I wanted,
at other times was ashamed to ask, and even then loved browsing
and the discovery of unexpected things. And I still hate to ask
questions and would rather flounder around on my own!

I do not want to carry this personal narrative further, though
I could thereby show the steps which one person took in becoming
a frequent user of libraries and information sources. I should,

Project No. 195 (Philadelphia: Drexel Inst. of Technology, Graduate School of
Library Science, 1964).

however, like to suggest that the study of the psychology of the library patron who is searching for information might be begun by each of you, using yourselves as guinea pigs, analyzing how *you* would ask for or search for information. A collection of such analyses might be a very useful contribution to our understanding of our users and their problems in communicating with us!

Donald Hunt asks, in the title of a recent article, "Where Is the General Reference Librarian and Bread-and-Butter Service?"[4] I should like first to discuss the "bread-and-butter" patron and his needs at the everyday level, and then to consider only briefly the more sophisticated user, since I am sure that many other participants in this conference will be concerned with the specialist and because I feel the common man is sometimes forgotten.

Who really are our users, our patrons, our clients, or whatever we wish to call them? There are surprisingly few broad studies of the persons who come to the library specifically for information, and there are a great many unanswered questions. Over the years, statistical analyses have been done by one library or another, and a few wider surveys have reported on percentages of students, housewives, clubwomen, teachers, children, businessmen, clerical workers, and day laborers, including their ages, sex, etc., who use some part of the library's services; but few of these have been specifically reference-oriented. The ambitious and frustrating survey[5] which was carried out by the Reference Services Division of ALA in 1955 and 1956, and for which results were belatedly published in 1961, included a question about types of public-library patrons, but the respondents were not asked to indicate the relative numbers of the different types, nor were the librarians asked how they had accumulated their data.

Many of the recent statewide library development surveys and plans, largely instigated by the Library Services Act, seem to be slanted toward studies of existing library services and resources and of the general nature of the population to be served. They give little information about the actual users of present services, and most of them show the librarians' analyses of needs, not direct reports from users. Although many of these state and regional surveys are limited to public libraries and do not apply specifically to reference services, some of them have been more inclusive in

[4]Donald R. Hunt, "Where Is the General Reference Librarian and Bread-and-Butter Service?" *College and Research Libraries*, 26:307-10 (July, 1965).

[5]American Library Association, Reference Services Division, Public Library Reference Survey Committee, *Reference Service in American Public Libraries Serving Populations of 10,000 or More; a Report of a Nationwide Survey* ("Occasional Papers," No. 61 [Urbana: Univ. of Illinois, Library School, Mar., 1961]).

their coverage of all types of libraries; and a few have been oriented entirely to reference services. One of these is the recently completed report by Guy Garrison, *A Statewide Reference Network for Wisconsin Libraries*.[6] This, too, investigates resources and services rather than actual patrons, except indirectly in connection with their demand for services.

One recent report, *Prospects for Library Cooperation in New York City*,[7] has investigated the actual users of many types of libraries in that city in considerable detail and seems to be a model which might be followed in other surveys. The announcement on March 3, 1966, of a new grant from the Council on Library Resources to implement the recommendations of this study is most encouraging! Other reports from individual libraries, showing statistics of types and numbers of patrons, appear from time to time, frequently in annual reports. Many of these have been digested in *Public Library Abstracts,* but not in a way that would make it easy to draw up any summary data for groups of libraries. For academic and special libraries, the materials seem even more fragmentary, even though it is unquestionably true that many individual special libraries know their patronage very well, and in academic circles librarians become thoroughly acquainted with at least some of their customers.

Many questions come to mind when considering the reference patron, the seeker of information within any type of library. There are the obvious ones of age, sex, occupation, educational status, etc. which should not be difficult to compile. Other examples, not so easy to answer and not well, if at all, covered in the literature, are these. What proportion of the library's patrons use reference/ information services today? (Mr. Clapp commented this morning that the "part of the public which has benefited from a dynamic library service is small indeed.") Is the finding, reported both by Los Angeles and the State of Wisconsin, that only about 27 percent of the people surveyed even knew that such services existed in libraries generally true?[8] Are our users a good cross section of the community served, or are some elements dominant? If so, why? Do reference services ever reach all levels of the population? Where do the users come from? (The New York study already mentioned shows most interesting patterns of reference

[6]Illinois, University, Library Research Center, *A Statewide Reference Network for Wisconsin Libraries,* by Guy Garrison; prepared for the Wisconsin Free Library Commission (Urbana, 1964).

[7]Nelson Associates, Inc., *Prospects for Library Cooperation in New York City: Planning for More Effective Utilization of Reference and Research Resources* (New York, 1963).

[8]Illinois, University, Library Research Center, *op. cit.,* p.13-14.

library use.) Have there been changes in the relative proportions of types of users in recent years? We are much aware of the student influx, but what about the remainder of our patronage? Has its makeup changed? Have adult patrons just been pushed out?

Have the increasing complexities of informational needs brought more patrons to reference departments and, if so, have all kinds of libraries felt the change, or only the special or the academic? Is there any evidence that our client of today is more skilled in the use of the library than the patron of twenty years ago—any evidence that our years of painful efforts at library instruction are bearing fruit? Do the students who used the reference services of libraries heavily in school come back to use them when they get out into the world? Has the increase in numbers of advanced and graduate students resulted in a comparable increase in the use of the academic library's reference resources? What about the patrons of our special libraries? As research and development programs have grown within an institution, have the number of users of the library increased at a similar rate? What has the effect of team research been on the people who use the library? Has there been appreciable delegation of literature and information searching to nonlibrary personnel? What does the growth of the many specialized information centers suggest about dissatisfaction with or ignorance of library reference/information services? And what about people who use and need information, but do not use the library and do not have access to a specialized information center? Where do they go?

I am sure there are many other questions which might be asked about the nature of our patrons. Some of the ones I have suggested could undoubtedly be answered by a few librarians who have made objective studies in specific situations. I suspect that many other reference librarians would tend to answer in general terms, although with nothing other than impressions to validate their replies.

It is, of course, difficult to separate investigations of the people who use the reference services from analyses of the questions they ask and the services they demand. Much of the knowledge we have of our clients is obtained indirectly by studying their requests. Many reference librarians consistently keep records of questions asked; others make spot checks or tally questions by type, difficulty, or time consumed. But what happens to these records? The whole sticky problem of analysis and evaluation of reference services was reviewed carefully by Samuel Rothstein in the January, 1964, issue of *Library Trends*,[9] already mentioned. It is interesting

[9]Samuel Rothstein, "The Measurement and Evaluation of Reference Service," *Library Trends*, 12:456-72 (Jan., 1964).

and perhaps significant to note that just about half of the references which Dr. Rothstein cites in his bibliography and discusses in the paper date from the 1940's or earlier. For instance, Dorothy Cole's study, "Some Characteristics of Reference Work,"[10] published in 1946, is still used as a basic analysis of types of questions and percentage of types of questions asked. I wonder if her proportions and types would hold up if a comparative study on a similar base were made today?

The Reference Standards Committee has been trying for years to get support for studies which might analyze reference questions, reference services, and statistics so that some standards for reporting and for comparison might be drawn. We are still waiting hopefully for word that the Committee's current proposal for the development of standards for reference service in large university and metropolitan public libraries will be funded.

Our professional literature frequently contains articles about questions asked in individual libraries, often written in a semihumorous vein, full of the kinds of questions which make librarians shudder. As an example I will mention only the most recent one I have seen, "The Answer?—That Is the Question," by G. W. Horner,[11] which was contributed to an otherwise serious group of essays honoring Barbara Kyle of the Association of Special Libraries and Information Bureaux. A careful study even of this type of data might be helpful in providing better information on how people ask questions. Many of the articles which attempt to be statistical show clearly that a very high percentage of information questions in any library—even the most specialized—are of the "bread-and-butter" factual variety. I have not found, however, any recently made broad study of questions by type or by subject that might show trends. Yet, with this kind of demand occupying such an important part of a reference librarian's time, should not an up-to-date study be made and some effort be put forth to maintain a continuing record of trends and needs? (It seems to me that our situation in facing this problem is somewhat similar to that in medicine when it comes to solving the mystery of the common cold. Just as research on spectacular, exotic, and more fatal diseases is so much more exciting, and also gets the financial support, so is the research emphasis in librarianship and related fields aimed at the fringes, and the humdrum is too much neglected.)

_____

[10]Dorothy E. Cole, "Some Characteristics of Reference Work," *College and Research Libraries,* 7:45-51 (Jan., 1946).

[11]G. W. Horner, "The Answer?— That Is the Question," *Journal of Documentation,* 21:252-55 (Dec., 1965).

What is the subject spread of questions asked today in a general reference library or a nondepartmentalized branch or in schools? Can we demonstrate by current statistics what topics are getting the most attention? In what areas are we finding our resources inadequate? And are they inadequate because sources do not exist, because we have not bought them, or because they are too expensive or specialized to be justified? What proportion of the questions asked by young people and children are school-oriented? Do children today have time just to be curious, or are even their nonschool questions the result of group stimulation, i.e., Boy Scouts, Girl Scouts, Junior Achievement, etc., rather than of individual interest? Have the smaller and nonspecialized libraries seen an appreciable growth in the number of difficult, technically oriented questions which have so preoccupied the documentalists? How about demands within these libraries for searches which extend beyond the walls of these institutions? What percent of the questions asked in academic or special libraries, or even in the information centers, are of the "bread-and-butter" type? Are the questions asked by the nonspecialist different in depth, in specificity, or in urgency than in the past? How has telephone reference service grown or changed? How about the need for interlibrary loan?

For some years Rose Phelps, before she retired from the University of Illinois, collected examples of reference questions and sources used, primarily from large public libraries, which were made available to reference teachers to try out on their students. Such a continuing compilation could be very useful today, not only in teaching but also for a careful study of trends and adequacy or inadequacy of material. If both the question as originally posed and what was actually wanted were recorded, a most revealing picture of the psychology of the inquirer and his interrogative habits might result.

The way research workers ask questions and seek information in libraries and elsewhere is being studied very seriously today by scientists and documentalists (and I intend to discuss this a little more fully later). But general reference librarians have contributed to very few such studies; and the nonresearch patrons have been almost completely neglected, though I am sure that every reference librarian could provide many examples of the strange way people of all ages "back in" to what they really want. As Dean Shera says:

Any experienced reference librarian can supply a long list of examples of stupid or improperly asked questions that have come across his desk, or entertain a listener for hours with stories of serendipity; but few people have ever stopped to

wonder, much less investigate, the relevance of these experiences for the understanding of the reference process.[12]

Should not we, as reference librarians, be doing something
about this? It is all very well to point out to librarians-in-training
how important it is to draw from the patron what he "really wants"
and to refer them to Margaret Hutchins' wise advice on the nature
of the reference interview or give them some of Tom Galvin's case
studies to discuss, but is this enough? How well do we understand
the psychology of our everyday users? Do children ask questions
of the librarian in a different way than do adults? Are they likely
to be more direct? Do people at various educational levels have
more or less ability in making their wants known? Do people who
use the public library approach the reference librarian differently
than do the patrons of academic or special libraries? Is there a
difference in the way questions are posed in various subject areas
by the nonspecialist? In the studies of scientists and engineers
doing research, there seems to be quite a measurable difference.
Is this true elsewhere? How about some careful use studies of
high school or college students, of children, of housewives, of
businessmen? Here, reference librarians could contribute valuable
data as well as subjective impressions.
    Many of the scientists who have been studied in connection with
"use patterns" have indicated very great reliance on asking the man
who knows. I wonder how many scientists so replying are already
well up in their fields— already well known and well acquainted
among their fellow specialists? Is the pattern the same for the
newcomer and the young person on the way up? Does he tend to
use published sources and the services of reference librarians
more? And what about the procedures of a specialist who is moving
out of his own field? What are his behavior patterns?
    Since other people are going to discuss in detail the levels of
service which are, or might be, offered to patrons, the adequacy or
inadequacy of reference materials, and the development of the best
systems to serve our patrons' needs and to organize the tremendous
amount of informative material with which we are being deluged, I
will not touch on these questions now. Basic to all of them, however,
is the need to know more about users and the way they go about satisfying their wants. Studies should be going on at all levels, not just
on the fringes.
    The many "use studies" already mentioned, which have appeared
in recent years, have centered largely in the fields of science and

---

[12] Jesse H. Shera, "Automation and the Reference Librarian," *RQ* 3:5
(July, 1964).

technology and have usually approached the problem by direct inquiry of individual research workers by means of interviews,
questionnaires, stopwatches, diaries, and, occasionally, by direct
observation. Some have been carried on by special librarians,
others by nonlibrarian investigators. This emphasis on the science-
technology field and on the research worker has come, of course,
because of the rapid growth of informational literature in these
fields; because of the inability of existing reference tools and personnel to cope with the kind of data needed; and because of the
pressures of economic and military competition, which have made
it seem worthwhile for industry and government to spend great
sums of money to try to alleviate the situation. Such studies were
well under way even before the arrival of the computer on the
scene; and as the possibilities of the use of mechanized methods
for part of the labor of information retrieval became apparent, the
need for better understanding of the relations among inquirer, inquiry, and indexing method became more obvious.

Mr. Clapp has mentioned the need for investigating the road-
block which the library catalog frequently makes between the
searcher for information and what he wants. Documentalists soon
discovered that "talking with" or "interviewing" that very large,
stupid, and inanimate object, the computer, was an even more difficult matter. After a number of years of playing around with gad-
getry, unrealistic codes, and impractical systems, they have come
down to earth and have returned to studies of the psychology of the
would-be user and of the best way to organize information for retrieval in order to bring about eventual user satisfaction.

Documentalists have begun to realize the importance of the
reference "interview" and the detailed analysis of what is wanted
by the inquirer. The barricade to interpersonal communication set
up by the computer has also started the investigation of the input
operation and indexing procedures which can most economically,
as well as adequately, put into the computer store the information
which, hopefully, may sometime be retrieved by a future user.
(Parenthetically, I should like to insert here that I am sure that
the "feedback" to the maker and the user of conventional indexing
and reference sources from the thesauri being generated for computer use and from the studies of semantics, syntax, roles, links,
and unconventional systems, should be of considerable use to reference librarians of the future, whether or not their services become mechanized.)

It has distressed many reference librarians, I know, to note
the immense sums of money which have gone into some of this
research and development. Is there any reference librarian who
has not thought wistfully of what *he* could do in developing his own

brainchild— a bibliographic literature guide, a special index, or a
research study—if he could only get his hands on just a little of
those funds? Perhaps we should be "trying harder," since we do
not seem to be in first place in the information retrieval game!
More than one person has suggested that documentalists are "re-
inventing the wheel," that they are continually rediscovering
things reference librarians already knew about the way people ask
for information, how they use the literature, and what sort of tools
they need. In a few cases, this may be true. But part of the fault
is ours. We have developed our "know-how" by rule of thumb,
through experience handed down among ourselves informally, and
we have not reported our data systematically or objectively. We
have been satisfied to accept twenty-year-old studies of users or
questions, to use nonsubject specialists in preparing many tools,
to report unverified impressions as facts, to grumble a little about
our basic tools but not to organize an all-out campaign to better
them.

Too few of us have persisted in working with the documentalists or ensured that our skills and experience were used when appropriate. We have been much too modest about the librarian's
part in what is now being called the "information transfer" process.
It is sad to see how seldom the librarian as a person or contributor
has been considered in these recent studies of information flow. If
the scientists reporting on how they sought and found information
mention the library at all, it is in terms of resources rather than
in consideration of the personal service given by the librarian. (I
wonder how many of the so-called "serendipitous" discoveries made
by research workers browsing through the library have really occurred because an interested librarian had quietly brought something to their attention? I can think of some in my own experience.)

Many special librarians have certainly been working closely
with documentalists, or have moved over into some of the activities
claimed by documentalists to be outside librarianship. It is re-
freshing to see that at last we begin to be aware that the reference
librarian is an important and contributing person in the process of
information transfer, and that the librarian should be studied both
as an intermediary in the process and as a user himself. Herbert
Menzel's article, "The Information Needs of Current Scientific
Research," concludes with this remark:

> In this paper I have emphasized the transmission of scientific
> information through means which make no obvious use of the
> librarian's contribution. I have pointed out that virtually any
> such transaction is only part of a chain of transactions. Other
> indispensable links of the same chain involve the identification,

locating, and retrieval of recorded data and documents for which the scientific researcher is indebted, more or less humbly and gratefully, to the skills of the librarian's profession.[13]

In the July, 1965, *RQ*, Pierre Papazian repeats in somewhat different words the idea which I had earlier tried to express in the same periodical.[14] Papazian says:

> Only a token amount of research has been done on the information librarian and his work. Yet the fact is that we know next to nothing about how a competent information librarian goes about finding the answer to a question. . . .
>
> . . . .
>
> It is now time for the information librarian to realize his potential through the analytical study of his own functional behavior. He will thereby greatly improve information services, and at the same time, enhance his professional status.[15]

Another encouraging statement was made last fall by Joseph C. Donohue of Informatics, Inc., in a paper given at the International Federation for Documentation Conference in Washington, D.C. He recommended three areas in which more research was needed: first, cataloging and classification; second, the structure of the information community; and third, reference methods. In connection with area number two, he said:

> Librarians, in search of information, explore and often describe in their professional literature the structure of the information community and the relations among its components. Such descriptions, properly studied, will contribute to the empirics of information science, and, properly quantified, can offer insights into the sociology of knowledge.

In commenting on reference methods, he added:

> The descriptive literature of reference service, and the skills passed on in its oral tradition contain the explanation of why a reference librarian is often more effective in literature search than our most advanced computer program. . . .

---

[13] Herbert Menzel, "The Information Needs of Current Scientific Research," *Library Quarterly*, 34:19 (Jan., 1964).

[14] Helen M. Focke, "The Place of the Reference Librarian," *RQ* 4:1-2,16 (Jan., 1965).

[15] Pierre Papazian, "Librarian, Know Thyself," *RQ* 4:7,8 (July, 1965).

In these and other areas librarians can offer a great body of information, hitherto accumulated in a pragmatic and largely uncritical manner.[16]

In summary, then, let me repeat my conviction that we do not know enough about our patrons, how their minds operate and what kind of things they need and ask for, to do a really good job of serving them. We have not gathered objective data continually or been as research conscious as we should be. It is vital that some of us, at least, break away from the pressures of the day-to-day grind, look at the whole reference/information pattern as we are doing this week, and then do something about it!

It seems to me that there are several important investigations which we, as reference librarians, should be carrying on right now. First, we should stop looking over the fence at greener pastures and stick our heads through the rails and begin to nibble at that green grass. And, second, we should take advantage of the studies on information-flow patterns and on user psychology which have already been done. We should use any of the facts or methods which have been developed, together with that "know-how" which everyone acknowledges that we have, to study patrons and their needs in many subject areas (not only in science), in various types of libraries, and at other than the specialist level.

It might then be possible for librarians to bring to the attention of the nonlibrarians who have been investigating methods of scientific information transfer some places where they may be off the track. As Dean Shera says in his review of the INTREX Conference held last summer:

...we regret the absence of the reference librarians, whose collective years of experience could have added much to the correction of assumptions and misconceptions about the nature of the information transfer process.[17]

Perhaps if more reference librarians had had an opportunity to participate, the librarian of 1975 (as envisioned in the INTREX report) would still have an important place in "the individual transaction between user and book" and not be relegated primarily to technical, nonpersonal processes![18]

---

[16]Joseph C. Donohue, *Librarianship and the Science of Information;* [paper] presented at the Conference of the International Federation for Documentation, Oct. 10-15, 1965 (Washington, D.C., 1965), p.7.

[17]Jesse H. Shera, "Librarians' Pugwash, or INTREX on the Cape," *Wilson Library Bulletin,* 40:361 (Dec., 1965).

[18]Planning Conference on Information Transfer Experiments, Woods Hole,

We should also study ourselves as intermediaries in the information transfer business, remembering that we, too, are users of the library and its materials; and we should work actively with the psychologists, the scientists, and others who are carrying on such research so that they become fully aware of what we can give and use it.

I don't want to suggest that research developments in the use of mechanized methods are unimportant, but we should also gather much more careful and objective data on the "bread-and-butter" references needs of our patrons. For "bread-and-butter" information, published data will be essential for a long time to come, and it would be foolish to query a computer for it, even if one were available. With realistic information at hand, we should then be able to enlist both the subject specialists working in information centers and the publishers to compile and make easily available in published and reasonably priced form the data which should be readily at hand and not just "on-line" through a computer.

How we can carry out these suggestions is another problem. Not all of the suggestions entail projects which can be carried on by typical committees, although, conceivably, committees can draw up plans for action. Some studies can be done by individual reference librarians who have a research bent (and time); others need team research, large group participation, and funds. I feel that, when properly formulated, they would be important enough to justify approach to fund-granting organizations. Certainly we should do all we can to further the work of the pertinent RSD committees and encourage them to crystallize projects worthy of outside support.

As a simple beginning, I would like to suggest that we could, and should, through the Reference Services Division, aided by the new Office for Research and Development, and perhaps the coming Division of Information Science and Documentation, establish a network of reporters, recorders, and data gatherers (not just a committee) which would build up a "data bank" of information on library patrons and on the questions they ask. This should be maintained on a continuing, not a spasmodic, basis, represent all sizes and types of libraries, and be available for future research of many kinds. Library schools could draw on the "bank" for material for research, and publishers could find out about needed materials. I can see RSD and its committees in a catalytic role, and also hope that within this conference some practical ideas and plans for expediting serious and continuing studies can be generated for the "bread-and-butter" needs, as well as for the esoteric ones.

Massachusetts, 1965, *INTREX: Report of a Planning Conference on Information Transfer Experiments,* ed. by Carl F. J. Overhage and R. Joyce Harman (Cambridge, Mass.: M.I.T. Pr. ₁1965₁), p.50.

A Spacious Closet of Reading

Marian M. Allen

Charles Lamb wrote of his sister Mary: "She was tumbled early, by accident or design, into a spacious closet of good old English reading, without much selection or prohibition, and browsed at will upon that fair and wholesome pasturage."[1]   He wrote that in 1821, more than fifty years before reference service was conceived, and some one hundred and fifty years before the time when virtually *no* enclosures of reading material could any longer be called spacious (just overcrowded!) and before selection by electronic device was dreamed of.

What are we proud of in the reference division of today, what are our present aims in this vast change that has transformed the reading world, and how well are we putting our theories into practice? Not too well, according to the authors of many entries in *Library Literature.* And there is rising concern about solving the problems quickly in the face of the double danger of the population explosion, which is itself being augmented by the increasing percent of those continuing their education, and, to use the now familiar phrase, of the geometric increase in library collections.

The urgency expressed in the current annual report of a university librarian is widely felt. He writes:

> The progress we have made in library collections and service in the past two or three years has been great, and

Marian M. Allen, Assistant Librarian in charge of Reference Services at the University of Rochester Library, has been a member of the Board of the ALA Reference Services Division and of the Joint Adult Services Division-Reference Services Division Committee on Orientation Project.

▶ [1] Charles Lamb, "Mackery End in Hertfordshire," in *The Essays of Elia and The Last Essays of Elia* (London: Oxford Univ. Pr., 1938), p.107.

continues to accelerate, but sometimes it seems like the
progress of a freight train which is being overtaken and
passed by a streamlined express. In 1964-65 we moved more
freight than ever before: we bought more books, catalogued
more titles; lent more, answered more questions, provided
more study space for longer hours. We carried on a number
of projects which amounted to rearranging the freight and
making repairs while in motion. We even made some headway
in the design and testing of automated techniques which could
eventually, so to speak, convert our freight into air express, a
conversion which would be difficult enough even if it did not
have to be done without stopping the train. Our resources are
greater than ever before—the holdings of the whole Library
system rose to 2,152,683 items—but their development is continually overtaken and passed by the expansion of advanced
study and research; we are less able to meet the needs of the
University than we were a year ago and much less able than
we were five years ago, because the need increases so rapidly.[2]

That the student population explosion is being felt in public
libraries as well as in educational institutions was clearly docu-
mented by the extraordinary interest and participation in the Conference within a Conference at the American Library Association
meeting in Chicago in 1963. The numbers of librarians who thronged
to those meetings and worked on committees were driven by a problem that is national in scope.
    Robert Downs begins an article on "Crisis in Our University
Libraries" by saying: "The great unanswered question in the minds
of American librarians ... is whether they can run fast enough to
stand still." He continues:

    There will doubtless be a temptation, as huge student en-
    rollments begin to swamp university campuses, to cheapen the
    quality of educational programs. Confronted by multitudes of
    students, some colleges and universities will resort to mass
    methods of instruction. ... Institutions concerned with produc-
    ing well-educated citizens, however, will avoid such techniques.
    In every way possible they will encourage independent work
    and study on the part of students, and for them the library will
    be the heart of the educational process. ...[3]

---

[2] Robert H. Blackburn, "Report," in University of Toronto, *President's
Report for the Year Ended June, 1965* (Toronto: Univ. of Toronto Pr., 1966),
p.158-59.
    [3] Robert B. Downs, "Crisis in Our University Libraries," *College and
Research Libraries*, 22:7, 10 (Jan., 1961).

This is a man who not only states a problem, but also comes up with some concrete solutions for it. His forthcoming book, scheduled for May publication, has the title *How To Do Library Research*,[4] and the *Publishers' Weekly* states that it tells students not only how to do research, but also how to use all library facilities, including special services, and their mechanics.

In thinking about the problems arising from the dramatically increasing quantities of materials, I remember, too, the urgency of the warning which Dean Shera gave at Lake Placid in the early fifties, at a New York Library Association conference. That, of course, was primarily on the flood of *scientific* literature. He predicted that, unless librarians recognized the need and began to cope with it realistically, research scientists would simply bypass libraries, and the result would be chaos.

As we all know, steps have been and are being taken to help meet that situation. But we also know that much remains to be done, and that it will be some time, if ever, before some fields of knowledge can be harnessed.

From the extensive library literature on the various levels of reference service, I have taken for consideration here those offered by Neal Harlow in an article, "Levels of Need for Library Service in Academic Institutions."[5] In order to identify and analyze needs, he uses the following terms:

> The "College" Library: the Library in the Program of General Education. . . .
> The "University" Library: the Library Serving the Maturing Student—Specialist—Scholar. . . .
> The Academic "Research" Library: the "Special" Library within the Academic Setting. . . .
> The "Special" Library: the Library Supporting Research and Development in Business, Industry, and Government. . . .

Many of the activities connected with service in these libraries, although labeled academic, are important in varying degrees in public libraries as well. The groundwork for them is important in elementary and secondary schools. Several years ago, the New York Library Association sent a questionnaire to colleges in the state, asking about the abilities of entering freshmen to use the library, and what librarians would like to see added or improved.

---

[4] Robert B. Downs, *How To Do Library Research* (Urbana: Univ. of Illinois Pr., 1966). 130p.

[5] Neal Harlow, "Levels of Need for Library Service in Academic Institutions," *College and Research Libraries*, 24:359-64 (Sept., 1963).

The general consensus was that the average ability of freshmen in library techniques was very low, that we would be grateful if we could be sure, as we were not then, of a knowledge on college entrance of the first basic principles of catalog entries and of those in the *Readers' Guide.*

It seems to me a reasonable objective to have those concepts clear by the end of secondary education. More complex entries will be met later, but the foundation is important, and time in college should not need to be spent on basic principles. However, it is also true that all libraries, if they are to face reality, must be prepared to give help at any level in individual cases. Nothing can be taken for granted, and, particularly in public libraries, people need reference help at all levels. Then, too, we must not forget the students here from the developing countries. They learn fast, but must have every assistance we can give them.

Last spring, the realization that public libraries needed some help in giving instruction to adults culminated in the formation in the American Library Association of the Joint Committee on Orientation, sponsored by the Adult Services Division and the Reference Services Division. The committee decided, as a first step, to find out through a questionnaire the methods and materials now being used for the instruction of individuals or groups of adults in the use of reference materials, the card or book catalog, and for general library orientation. The questionnaires were sent last fall to all public libraries in the United States. They asked whether the librarian felt a need for such an investigation and, if so, for concrete suggestions. About one third were returned, and the replies were almost unanimous in approval of such a project and indicated, with notable exceptions, a lack of satisfactory material. Some of the comments were:

> We are returning the enclosed questionnaire primarily to encourage the ASD/RSD Joint Committee to "study public library orientation of adults and develop a program of action." The fact that we have nothing new to answer to questions II through IV illustrates clearly the need for a positive answer to question V.... The tremendous growth of the _____ County Library has precluded the development of other [than traditional] techniques on a system-wide basis.

> Yes—definitely. Too many of us lack staff and facilities for doing a well-planned program or well-designed materials, alone. This seems a *general* need and if it can be done centrally instead of differently and individually all over the country, we are making what man-power we have count for more.

There is a group of adults needing instruction, but who are too shy to ask.

Many adults appreciate anything which helps them to become do-it-yourselfers.

We find an appalling lack of understanding [on the part of adults trying to use the library]. Help to individuals is a *part* of the answer, but surely not all of it. Pulling our hair has not helped. We eagerly await results of this survey.

I do not know the best way. I don't even have a *poor* way. Please have some informed committee work on these things. I have not been much help to you—I hope you can be more help to me in your report.

Perhaps I might add that the committee's next very practical step is to study various mechanical devices at a preconference this summer in New York, to be followed by preconferences on orientation at San Francisco in 1967 and at Kansas City in 1968.

Now to go back to some phases of service in academic libraries. Reference service at the first, or college, level usually includes a manual which serves as a guide to collections and ways of locating material, augmented by personal and group instruction in the use of the card catalog, bibliographies, and indexes. Perhaps an ideal to keep in mind here might be the need to strengthen the student's ability to work at an independent level, to prepare him not only to function successfully in his academic life, but also to give him the mechanics which he can carry on into his adult life and thus develop the ability to "work out his own problem, ... to select, sift, organize, and evaluate information." This is important in the fast-changing world of today. Sydney Harris wrote recently:

It is no accident that, for the first time, the prestigious Massachusetts Institute of Technology has appointed a president who is neither a scientist nor a technician. Or that business schools, such as those at Harvard and Columbia, have shifted their emphasis from the technical aspects of business administration to a broader program of liberal arts. ... More and more, the function of the specialist is being taken over by the machines; it is the "generalist," who can make decisions based on an imaginative projection of the future, we so desperately require to keep the wheels turning.[6]

This, then, should be kept clearly in mind as we plan our approach to helping the college student. He has to have the knowledge

[6]Sydney Harris, "Strictly Personal," *Chicago Daily News* (Jan. 26, 1966), p.14, col. 3.

and develop the ability to find information if he is to live in a
changing world flexibly, intelligently, and creatively, and to think
independently. Learning the techniques of using library material
may not be considered an intellectual activity (is learning to read
intellectual?), but I think it is part of becoming a literate person
today. When traveling in a strange country, for instance, Russia,
it is good to be able at least to read signs and not be entirely dependent on others to point out the way. Most of the time, we are
happy to depend on a cab to get us quickly to our destinations in a
city, but we *can* find ourselves without a cab or without confidence
in the driver. So this ability to select material might be thought of
not only as leading to personal satisfaction, but also as a safeguard
against possible totalitarianism, which is inherent in some systems
of rapid supply of reading material and information. So much for
the philosophy of the matter. Let me turn to several concrete examples of work being done.

The several colleges in the Rochester area, I think, give a fair
example of some of the reference needs existing throughout the
country today, illustrating the "present status." Those libraries
are using, in part, traditional practices long established. But some
are expanding rapidly in size; two, other than the University of
Rochester, are anticipating student bodies of perhaps 8000-10,000
in the near future. They need effective methods.

One library has given up the practice of visiting classrooms
with a few reference books carried along for illustration. It was,
as many others have found, too time-consuming and frustrating in
the end result. At the moment it is giving no group instruction.
Another is using lectures with slides and accompanying sound
track, made at the institution. It has no separate space for group
instruction in the library but is following the plan of offering the
lectures, along with a supplementary workshop, on a volunteer
basis during a college vacation, a time when it is able to use
the library freely without disturbing readers. The instructors,
as well as the students, give up vacation days! Adequate space
will be available on a new campus which is being developed. Several librarians speak of the need for a lecture room in the library
building, close to the catalog and reference material. We at the
University of Rochester look forward to such a facility in the new
library wing. Two of the institutions had written to ALA for film
material, but did not find just what they wanted.

In 1964 I participated in another study with a geographical
basis—a study of the four large universities of western New York:
Cornell, Syracuse, Buffalo, and Rochester. We learned what each
was doing, and we discussed what we would like to see at each institution. The report of the study, entitled *The Second Kind of*

Knowledge,[7] included consideration of various reference instruction devices which could be useful: motivational and instructional films, film strips, slides, programmed instruction, materials for overhead projection, video tapes, and handout sheets, all of which would take time and the effort of some experienced person or group to prepare. The need was considered great at that time, and, with the increasing size of each entering class, it becomes more intense. Implementation did not follow that study, because funds had been provided for the survey only.

Another personal experience may illustrate how vulnerable a program may be to the pressures of the curriculum. For a number of years, our reference staff worked closely with students enrolled in the freshman English course. We gave assistance with the usual long paper, but preceding that was a course unit on reference materials. This turned into something similar to a junior course in reference, based on the "where would you look first" approach. I think that the unusual impetus for really significant achievement in the project was gained from the type of questions set the students by the faculty member in charge of all the English 101 sections. His brilliance and wide approach caught their interest so surely that they *wanted* to know how to find answers. Some students told us that they spent fifteen or more hours on the problem, and at the end many, if not most, students had changed from hesitant new arrivals, hopefully or defensively looking for *Bartlett* as one thing familiar in this strange wilderness of 15,000 reference books, to persons who felt at ease in their surroundings, who felt that now they could "work the system."

Our part, of course, was not to find answers, but to put questions: where have you looked, what kind of reference source do you think might help, and so on. And to supplement this, we not only had Winchell on hand, but also a very practical display on 6-inch by 10-inch cards which divided up, by form and subject, scores of subjects, with each card suggesting a list of authorities on that subject.

The display was (and is) in horizontal cases in front of the center reference desk, and the student could range through the cards considering the possibilities for the subject area he wanted to investigate, turn to the wheeldexes on the center reference desk to get the call numbers with any special location, and start the search. I will admit that we began the display as something of a defense measure, after most of the thousand or so students involved

---

[7] Luella Snyder, *The Second Kind of Knowledge* (Syracuse, N.Y.: Inter-university Program in Teacher Education and School of Library Science, Syracuse Univ., 1964). 44p.

seemed to descend on us the first year at the same time. A stag-
gered time schedule, plus a more organized approach the following
year, changed the project into an intensely busy but rewarding
experience.

Two years ago, the whole freshman course as such was dropped
—and with it, the introduction to reference materials, as well as the
long paper. The particular faculty member went on to other responsibilities; the freshmen, because of their generally high scholastic
ability, were directed into more advanced courses. Our department
was asked to prepare a special English handbook to help fill the gap.
But the welcome word has just recently been received of the deter-
mination to incorporate somehow into the curriculum at least part
of the reference instruction given formerly. We have in the meantime kept the display cases active with their breakdown of materials
ready for all users, as part of a plan for having as many self-help
arrangements as possible. Special classes and groups ask to have
talks given to them by the reference department, and mimeographed
sheets on various aspects of reference are ready at all times to be
given out; otherwise, individual assistance, with its limited coverage, is the order of the day.

Perhaps I have spent too much time on reference assistance at
the college level. But I feel that there is a real need here, that this
is the time when a firm foundation for independent thinking can be
established. Also, much that can, and should be, worked out for use
here is of value elsewhere. Any previous training in the use of
libraries is good, but the use of a collection at an academic level
can not be adequately experienced outside it. The transition from
high school to college is not automatic, and the library needs to
play its part in that period. May I quote Dean Shera:

> Yet the qualitative problem of education must be solved if our
> technology is not to create an environment in which mankind
> is unable to survive.
>
> One cannot (within the limitations of the present essay)
> consider all the weaknesses in American education, but cer-
> tainly one of the most serious is the high degree of functional
> illiteracy, even at the college level. . . .
>
> A school . . . is an institution for promoting the growth,
> development, and enrichment of man's intellectual powers. It
> is the proving-ground of the mind, and the library is its arse-
> nal. We suffer defeat in the increasing battle against ignorance
> largely because we have not learned how to use its weaponry.[8]

---

[8] Jesse H. Shera, "Staffing Library Services To Meet Student Needs . . . ,"
in *Libraries and the Organization of Knowledge;* ed. and with an introd. by D.
J. Foskett (Hamden, Conn.: Archon Books, 1965), p.198-99.

At the second level, that of subject specialization, assistance is also vital today. Again, library literature is full of discussion of the need for subject specialists, with occasional mention of the value of the general reference librarian. As I see it, both are needed, and I hope that, in some ideal state, both will be made available in generous numbers.

Until that day comes, may I simply cite again as illustration two simple items which we find helpful in general reference at the University of Rochester? We have ready for all graduate students mimeographed lists of the bibliographical sources available for each subject field. Each list runs to several pages, and the sources are grouped usually as comprehensive, continuing, and period, with call numbers and actual locations given. We have been told, especially by graduate students coming from other institutions, that this one device cuts several weeks of groping for sources as they begin their work.

Another means used to inform and open areas of material, to faculty as well as to graduate students, is mimeographed lists of the nonbook indexes which are available in the reference department. The lists are annotated and are grouped into five subject areas. The natural tendency for many students to use only what they know about or have had recommended by a fellow student or faculty member can leave untouched many resources ready and waiting in most well-stocked academic libraries. Our lists run to a total of about 110 entries, so those students who have depended primarily on hearsay, on such universally recommended sources as *PMLA*, or on the special slant of an individual faculty member cannot help but have their horizons extended.

For the third level, that of service at the scholarly level, may I begin with a definition from Mr. Clapp's recent book, *The Future of the Research Library*. "Stated in the simplest terms, the function of the research library is to enable inquirers to identify library materials relevant to their inquiries and to supply them with copies of these materials for their use."[9] And Rutherford Rogers wrote, in a paper presented to the ACRL Reference Librarians Section in Chicago on January 21, 1949, that an "analysis of the big problems of reference service indicates that they are directly related to the big problems of reference and research libraries." In discussing those problems he sounded an alarm similar to that of Dean Shera on the scientific information-retrieval crisis. Rogers said: "I take the position that we have already entered such a critical period in research library administration that either we shall meet the

---

[9] Verner W. Clapp, *The Future of the Research Library* (Urbana: Univ. of Illinois Pr., 1964), p.11.

fundamental issues facing us, or routines will not matter." Later
in the paper he remarked:

> Many a research library director is alarmed that more
> and more highly trained people work behind the scenes as cat-
> alogers while insufficiently trained or untrained people work
> with the public. It is much easier to see a room full of uncat-
> aloged books than it is to evaluate the harm done to your service
> by lowering the quality of people who wait on the public....
> More serious than cost is the inadequacy of the card cat-
> alog as a subject tool. The head of a large research library
> writes me that the "... card catalog is already too unwieldy
> for untrained readers to use, and by untrained readers I mean
> not only college students but graduate students and our general
> public as well.
> ... An advanced reader often finds our subject headings out-
> moded. This situation grows worse each year. We, and other
> libraries, are still using headings drawn up 10 to 20 years ago."

This was written in 1949. Mr. Rogers continued:

> The subject catalog has had its day and the answer to our
> problem is subject bibliography created on a national or in-
> ternational scale. We have not begun to explore the problems
> of adequate subject bibliography.... Now is none too soon to
> take concerted action along these lines....
> . . . .
> If we are going to acquire huge amounts of materials, we are
> obligated to make them useful to the scholar wherever he may
> be. How can the individual library interpret this mass of ma-
> terials except by subject bibliographies rather than through a
> single subject or classified catalog in Washington, D.C.?
> . . . .
> We must undertake integrated planning with respect to all
> our problems ... we need an intelligent plan with the whole-
> hearted backing of our own profession.[10]

The fourth and last level of reference service in my outline is
that of producing actual information. There are many librarians

[10]Rutherford D. Rogers, "Administrative Problems of Reference and Re-
search Libraries," in *References Services;* selected by Arthur Ray Rowland
("Contribution to Library Literature," No. 5. [Hamden, Conn.: Shoe String
Pr., Inc., 1964]), p.61-70.

today who would like to see all reference librarians ready and able to offer that kind of help as successfully as the special librarian has long done. And why not?

Samuel Rothstein, now Director of the School of Librarianship at the University of British Columbia, has given various evaluations of reference service over recent years, with devastatingly gentle or gently devastating effect. He is a remarkably clear-sighted mentor and would not have us set our standards too low. At a meeting of the Reference Services Division in Montreal, he listed the various levels of reference work as: instruction in the use of books and libraries; guidance in the choice of books; and information service, "getting information out of books." He identified the theories on which these services rest as "minimum," "middling," and "maximum," with the librarian functioning at the top level more as a special librarian or "information officer," or perhaps even a documentalist. Rothstein is one of those who feels that reference librarians as a whole should step up service at this level materially.

He goes on to say (and I hope that I am not doing him an injustice by selecting a number of his statements which concern us here): "In the libraries that serve scholars and research scientists, the case for an amplified reference service is even stronger... research workers stand in growing *need* of a full-scale reference service."

At a later point, Rothstein continues:

> You will have already noticed that, in the foregoing analysis, I have leaned rather heavily on the reference librarian's potential contribution to *scientific* research. It is certainly true the subdivision of labor implied in this relationship is more readily applicable to the physical sciences and technology than it is to research in the humanities and social sciences....
>
> Yet I refuse to admit that the reasoning that makes an amplified reference service feasible and desirable for scientific research does not extend to other fields of investigation....

As "food for thought," Rothstein suggested several possibilities for solutions to the problems that he raised:

> 1. Library budgets *can* be increased—perhaps several times over—without putting the slightest strain on the economy of either the United States or Canada....
> 2. The reference services—and especially the information service—can get a large share of the existing library budget.... it may well be that we spend too much money on our technical processes and not enough on our public services. (By the way,

I happen to be in charge of technical processes at my library.)

3. There seems to be sound reason for hope that advances in library technology can produce savings which could be applied to the expansion of information services. Much of our cataloging, circulation, and acquisitions work can be mechanized, and for that matter, we are promised machines for "information retrieval" too. In any case the point is the same; the library is freed to concentrate on the really intellectual tasks in librarianship, and prominent among them the information service.

4. A foundation—and of course the Council on Library Resources springs promptly to mind—might be persuaded to sponsor adequate demonstrations of amplified reference service, say, adding a dozen subject specialists to each of a number of public and university libraries.... The Carnegie Corporation "research librarianships" constituted a test of sorts, but were hardly conclusive. A full-scale experiment is now in order.

Later, in summarizing, Rothstein states: "When reference service and particularly an information service became established as a regular part of American library practice, it really constituted a new dimension in librarianship; we began to deal in knowledge and not just volumes."[11]

So what is my position for the reference/information service of the future? It is in every instance affirmative. I subscribe to all the progress possible in the field of mechanization through the full range of machine readable devices, teaching machines, films, and the most exciting and extensive of all, the prospect of going "'on-line' to the national [and even international] reference system" which we heard discussed this morning—devices and systems which can inform, supply increasing amounts of materials, and advance dramatically the bibliographical services available. I subscribe to the training and increased use of subject specialists to meet the vital needs of the growing armies of specialists in our world today. I subscribe to the theory and practice of "information officers." Information we certainly need today, and quickly. But I also subscribe with equal fervor to the continuing presence and activity of the general reference librarian who can interpret, evaluate, and act as catalyst between the library user and all the recorded knowledge available anywhere. This in itself is a special service. As Dean Shera put it: "The true role of the librarian, then, is to

---

[11] Samuel Rothstein, "Reference Service: the New Dimension in Librarianship," in *Reference Services, op. cit.*, p.37-45.

mediate between book and reader, and the human factor that is the librarian can never be eliminated."[12]

In the philosophy of education, there are those who feel that it is good to put the full professor who enjoys teaching in classes for undergraduates, leaving assistants for some of the advanced work. I feel that the best and most experienced librarian should similarly be available at the college level and for work with the public. He need not—indeed, should not—spend all his time on the front line. He no doubt would have one or two specialties of his own, as the full professor does. But he should *not* be so submerged in administrative and/or special projects that he is kept from his public. Teaching devices would save his time from the dull, repetitious details of instruction.

One specialty might be to act as an "information officer"; another, to set up teaching machines which would not repel the user because of their trite treatment. He might help develop anything that looms on the horizon for future time-saving techniques. He would know about and make use of the various systems now appearing: MEDLARS, COBOL, INTREX, MARC, and so on. However, a substantial portion of his time would be spent in contact with the public. I would add that increasing the percent of the "full professor" librarians out front would help solve the recruiting problem and ameliorate the fundamental problem of staff shortage. It would be one way of shouting our wares and advertising the better mousetrap referred to by Mr. Clapp in his opening address.

I quoted at the beginning from the annual report of the librarian of the University of Toronto. To set our sights on the whole picture of what we as librarians are a part of, may I end with this year's report from Harvard? Mr. Pusey writes:

> Made weary by a seemingly endless recital of needs during recent years, members of the Board of Overseers might well ask: Just what is this mission [of the University]? Is it anything that can be accomplished? The answer, which you know as well as I, is, of course, both yes and no.
>
> Stated simply, Harvard's purpose is to conduct research and to produce a continuing flow of highly trained people for a wide variety of careers; though at the college level, it is perhaps rather simply to provide rich opportunity to select individuals for intellectual and personal growth.
>
> But if we look more closely, surely we must agree it is

---

[12] Jesse H. Shera, "What Lies Ahead in Classification." in *Libraries and the Organization of Knowledge, op. cit.,* p.137.

more than this. Can it indeed be anything less than to contribute to the best of our ability to the furtherance of civilized life?[13]

As librarians, we should be ready to subscribe to this purpose —with one change. We cannot really be successful in our profession unless we change one phrase and aim to do our utmost to provide rich opportunity, not to select individuals, but to *individuals* —ultimately, *all* individuals—for their intellectual and personal growth. To this end, we can dedicate ourselves.

---

[13] Harvard University, *The President's Report, 1964-1965* (Cambridge, Mass.: Harvard Univ., Jan. 10, 1966), p.18.

Reconstruction of Library Services

Leonard H. Freiser

Some years ago, I rather facetiously had put into print a little piece called "Requiem for the Public Library,"[1] in which I laid the public library to rest in 1973. That was after working for a period of time with the public libraries and seeing what they were doing in the face of all the opportunities they had with students—they were throwing students out. And now that I have been working in the field of education for five years, I am going to extend another requiem today. I should say that everything I am going to say today is in the nature of a question, not a statement. I will address my remarks to the rather modest title, "Reconstruction of Library Services."

I will begin with the individual. As a child, he looks at stars; he plays and listens to stories. He sings. He has a natural drive to learn and to modify. He responds to his world. More important, he uses tools to make his world responsive to him. The drives to learn and to modify within the boy continue in the man in the manner of Newton's first law of motion; they go on unless they are compelled to change by forces impressed thereon. Our job, and our society's job, is to keep these drives moving, without letting the forms that our solutions take, such as schools and libraries, become deflecting forces.

Educational practices are under constant criticism, and we hear about innovation and reform. But what I question are not

Leonard H. Freiser, with experience in public library work, has taught in the fields of public library administration and music. He is now Chief Librarian of the Toronto Board of Education, the services of which he has described in many articles.
▶ [1] Leonard H. Freiser, "Requiem for the Public Library, 1834-1973," *Library Journal*, 87:3623-25 (Oct. 15, 1962).

practices or methods; I question the institutions of education: public schools on the one hand and public libraries on the other.

The major forces which eventually led to these two institutions gained momentum with the invention of movable type. Gutenberg and Ford represent a repetitive, compartmentalized and mechanical technology—technology which led to factories and schools and, in turn, required them in order to flourish. We are no longer in the nineteenth century of mechanical technology, but are well into the electric twentieth. Our sense of place, of time, and of space has changed. Yet we continue to seek today's educational solutions within the framework of yesterday's educational institutions.

My thesis is this: at a time when our own nervous systems are being extended by electronics and our world is becoming smaller and less compartmentalized, our solutions in education will be environmental—not separate solutions in separate departments, but community solutions for all to use and responsible to all.

My proposal for an approach to a solution is to take one community and replace both the public school and the public library with a resource center. This would be a campus or urban building complex with total information services in print, radio, telephone, film, video, computer; with various facilities for doing things in studios, shops, laboratories, conference rooms, playrooms, stadium, theater; and with a professionally heterogeneous staff, which would be both permanent and drawn from the community. Underlying the flexibility of this center is the possibility that information may become an electric utility, reaching into homes with film discs, telephone-computer circuits, video, and print-out. The center could also extend itself through mobile units, the mails, and special branches which could be set up and knocked down according to community requirements. As a side advantage, the resource center would resolve the question of school library and public library duplication.

This, then, is my method and my proposal: first, to look at the individual, his society, and his technology; second, to reconstruct library services (by which we mean educational services) by creating a responsive environment.

There is little new here in the way of theory. Basic criticisms of educational organization and a desire to come to grips with today's technology and the unique requirements of individual students occur not only in the works of Paul Goodman and R. Buckminster Fuller, but also in conversations with thousands of working schoolmen. However, almost without our awareness, our instinct for providing service has been in a tug of war with our buildings and our methodology. Our point of view is harnessed in concrete.

Politicians speak more truth than they realize when they point to what they consider to be unnecessary duplication in having both school libraries and public libraries in the same neighborhood. It is an old story. On the one hand, there is the desire to save on taxes; on the other, there is the fact that putting public libraries in schools has not worked. Besides, there can never really be enough books for children. Agreed. These arguments, however, are rooted in and accept the underlying assumptions on which our present schools and libraries operate. The question of duplication is not really resolved, because the reverse side of the argument is that present organization makes duplication necessary.

The individual is not fundamentally interested in school and library buildings nor in the practices made necessary by the institutions. He is concerned with doing and learning, reading what is readable, viewing what is viewable, listening, thinking, making, dreaming, talking, and meeting. Let us reconstruct our services for him—not from the ground up, but from the sky around.

There are, of course, many signs around us of reconstruction of services to people. The Peace Corps and the poverty programs are attempts at transcending institutional rigidity and approaching the "I-thou" relationship. Progress has been made in the revitalization of the urban center and in the search for more sensible suburban arrangements. We are approaching health and economic security through Medicare and a guaranteed annual income. Within the structure of our schools there are questions and changes. The nongraded school, the movement away from tests and marks, the search for the flexibility to accommodate individuals and change and to provide for independent search and learning, and the library-centered school are all forerunners of reconstruction.

Underlying this activity are the influences of an electronic environment and a shift in the concept of education, which cause the definitions of school, library, entertainment, and museum to merge and to change. Every child has two educational environments. One is the school; the other is everything else. It is fashionable to say that children learn more out of school than they do in. What is overlooked —although it is there to be seen, like the puzzle with the hidden face in the trees—is that schools are influential less in what they teach than in what is between the lines. In electronics this is called noise. The school's social structure, attitudes, and double-standard approach to reality are what come across powerfully to most students.

A serious time lag exists between schools and education because our present organization is incompatible with mid-century society and technology. Public schools and public libraries have performed miracles in the first half of this century; but if they continue as they are, it will take a miracle for them to achieve success in the second

half. Our young children, through television, observe the migratory
and courting habits of birds, circumnavigate the world, and go into
space before they enter kindergarten. Quite early in life they learn
to be selective, accepting and rejecting programs according to the
holding power of the production. A growing difference between our
generation and our children's is that we saw our schools as a universe of information, a mystery box requiring us to find the right
key. Our children, however, are in themselves centers of information universes. A curriculum for these children is their own
search for curriculum. A school for these children is an environment responsive to their search.

In proposing a resource center for all ages to replace both
public school and public library, I am not suggesting an answer but
a test of a hypothesis. It is this: that the major job of our society
—education—cannot be fragmented by institutions, by institutional-
ized curricula, or by institutional categorization of people; that
education, to be consistent with our society, must be (and, with our
technology, can be) tailored for the individual; that education requires total information resources and the full or partial services
of a variety of professionals and craftsmen; that success in education rests on free, not compulsory, activity; that the special function
of the librarian is to ensure that total information resources in all
media are easily and universally accessible and disseminated; that
the librarian shares with the teacher a responsibility for learning
and shares with the publisher a responsibility for dissemination;
and that a resource center, replacing both the public library and
the public school, can provide a highly responsive environment for
the intensive and progressive education of individuals.

I have a suspicion that in replacing the public school and the
public library with a resource center I am being conservative.
Perhaps it represents a halfway point—an exploratory vehicle with
built-in obsolescence. "There are children playing in the street
who could solve some of my top problems in physics," said Robert
Oppenheimer, "because they have modes of sensory perception
that I lost long ago."[2] The resource center is an environment in
which children become participants in discovery.

I am tempted to expand my earlier description of the center
and to discuss some of the questions which obviously arise. But
when a thing like this is nailed down, it becomes impossible to
move. However, there are elements of this idea in practice scattered around. It is from the successful development of one of the
elements that I have come to my present stand. This is the

[2] Robert Oppenheimer, quoted in Herbert Marshall McLuhan, "Address at
Vision 65," *American Scholar*, 35:204 (Spring, 1966).

random-access information service to students and teachers in the Toronto school system. Here we got further verification that people respond significantly to this mode of communication. Our students feel linked in, part of the circuit.

I believe most of you know what we do, but, in summary, I would like to make a few points. The library of the Educational Centre, the curriculum center of the Toronto School Board, with 105,000 children and 4500 teachers, started some five and one-half years ago as a professional library. After a year and a half, there was exploration to see what the requirements of the adults in this educational community were. It began as a library for adults; for teachers, architects, psychologists, and maintenance people. Of course, we discovered that these were workaday people, and that they usually required information on what other people were doing in their fields. We set up an information service for them which, quite briefly, is this. They can either come to us or phone us (usually they phone us), and our staff, which now numbers eighty with fifteen professionals working on the information service alone, goes through the entire literature pertaining to the subject of the request. It gets the information, whether from the sixty or eighty indexes that are available in our own center, from our own 3000 to 4000 periodicals, or from the Library of Congress or the University of Toronto library. Our staff policy is to get the information, Xerox it, and send it out.

The other part of the service consists of getting information out in advance, scouring the journals, keeping in touch by telephone with people in the field, writing reports (we have several professional writers to do this), putting out lists of contents, and letting people know what is going on in their fields. These have been the two functions of our information service. Up to now it has been giving total information service only on what is in print, but presently it is working toward all media response. But we in education are not concerned with the working adults, the employees at the Board of Education. We are concerned primarily with students. If the time of a teacher is valuable, the time of a student is triply valuable. He is a child but once, and this is the most important time of his life. It is quite simple to extend to students this service which we have been giving to teachers and officials and trustees. Here we do exactly the same thing, except that the teachers of libraries call in the students' requests; however, we are moving toward a phase where the students will be able to telephone their own requests.

Now I would like to touch upon some remarks which were made here about teaching people how to use libraries. Those of you who know me know that I may not agree with everything said. Why?

None of you could use my library. I would not trust any of you to
do the kind of job that our reference librarians do. *I* can't use my
library. I have been out of touch with the reference area for two
years; and if you are not in the field, if you are not working with
the ever changing sources and with the ever changing people in the
field (because we are constantly phoning people outside to verify
what they say in print and also to get further information), if you
are not in touch with all this, you cannot do a decent piece of work.

It takes us six months to train a good librarian in our library;
it used to take about nine months to a year to train one for the reference section in a public library. This is why I question the "teach
them to do this" kind of thing. What can you get from the *Readers'
Guide* or the *Social Sciences and Humanities Index* or, for that
matter, from forty indexes if you do not know your field? What do
you expect children to get from any kind of instruction? The people
who need the most information are our three- to five-, eight- to ten-
to twelve-year-olds, and they can use it. Our secondary-school
students have been using university and post-university level information. When we ask the teachers whether this is over the students'
heads, they say, "No, anything less than this would be a waste of
time. They react in a very real way; they come to grips with real
things."

This is where our information is needed, and students and
librarians, unless they are trained in a particular field, are unable
to get it. In a certain sense, just as education should be an interest
of all of us, a discipline of all of us chosen voluntarily, so should information science or reference work or librarianship, whatever
you care to call it. In this sense, all of us should have a very keen
interest in what information is today, because this is one of the
major intellectual questions of our time. Students should be aware
of what information is: how it is communicated, what its sources
are, and who controls these sources. In this sense, I say students
should be aware of information, but not of the specific bibliographic
techniques, which, by the way, change from library to library. In
a certain sense, if we are content with allowing students to go forth
with a minimum of peripheral information, we demean our own
profession by saying that this is all one has to know to get information. On the other hand, if this is not true, and some of you may
question me on this, the other side of the point is that the student
does not need as much information as we are able to give him. If
he learns a few things in the *Readers' Guide* or other indexes, he
will be able to get as much information as he deserves. I disagree
with this completely.

To sum up what I have said: the starting point for the reconstruction of library service should be some rather concrete images

of what each person ought to have from an ideal service. What does it look like to the individual? What does he get? Work from this, rather than from a system down to the individual; work from the individual toward an organization of services. There are a number of factors we obviously have to consider. We must begin to understand what technology means to us. We must not look into the technical or the gimmick or the gadget aspects of new machinery; instead, we must begin to examine the philosophical implications of the modes of communication that we have. As public librarians, we have always been aware and must continue to be aware of the way people live, the way they work, their urban and suburban patterns, the way they receive information and services. That people need not come to libraries, that libraries should go to people, is an old story with us. Moreover, we must be aware of what is going on in education.

Education is becoming one of the most dominant power factors in our life today. Therefore, when we speak of education today, we are no longer referring to the schools; we are referring to people from the ages of one year straight up to ninety. Money is going into education as it has not gone into public library service in the past and perhaps not into other library services, and I would caution all of you to be very well aware of the implications of the new education movement which has been going on for a number of years. We also have to be aware of the implications of governmental control, whether we are interested in local control or central control, national control or international control, the whole structure under which any of the services which may develop will form.

Now a few words from practical experience. I think it would be trite to say that planning precedes hardware. You cannot start with machines; you cannot start with hardware or computers. You have to start with a philosophy, with objectives. In a way, you have to set up working models, handmade; carve the car in wood and see how it looks before you put it up for production. I think we have achieved in Toronto, working by hand, by very, very traditional library methods—the same methods we used in the Brooklyn Public Library reference section—a working model of a random-access information service to students. There are no computers. The most advanced technology we use is the telephone. The Xerox 914 makes our service possible, of course.

I have already mentioned that I would recommend a resource center to be tried in one place—a total environment, an educational library-information environment to which people come voluntarily. The legal requirements of compulsory attendance in school could be overcome by declaring the entire community a school. The success of this resource center would depend upon how many people it could attract and how many people it could keep. The resource center would have teachers, librarians, musicians, lathe operators, if you will. It would also have all the facilities necessary for doing things: for participation, for playing in orchestras, for painting, for typing, for independent study, or for group discussion. I have already discussed this, but there are two theoretical points that I would like to make.

I would like to suggest to you that our responsibility for information lies not only in providing information or disseminating information before requested, but also in considering the responsibilities that we have to information itself. It is completely irresponsible to give out the most up-to-date piece or the most up-to-date bibliographical reference which may, in fact, be inaccurate. It is irresponsible for somebody to give me an article saying that it costs five dollars to get a particular service when, in fact, it costs six dollars. Even though that article was received in the library today, it might be discovered by a telephone call that the price has been changed. We are not in the business of giving out printed materials. We are in the business of communicating real information. I would suggest that during your deliberations you consider all of the possibilities of publication, of the dissemination of information from primary sources rather than from secondary sources, namely, bibliographical sources.

This brings me to my last point—the nature of information. It is not enough to get at the bibliographical material which we need and will continue to need. It is not enough to get at a lot of inaccurate or misleading information more rapidly through a computer. We must look into the philosophic aspects of what information is. Let me give you a specific example in the field of education. If you were to put down a hundred articles on this table, a hundred different ones on the field of education, at least eighty, and I am being kind, would have to be crossed off as articles which should not have been written at all; they say absolutely nothing. In looking at the other twenty, you will see things of great interest, but the most you can get from these articles is that apparently something is going on somewhere and this is the way one person reports it.

I am not speaking, by the way, of theory or of philosophy; I am not speaking of what belongs in print. I am speaking of descriptions of programs which are the heart of the educational literature for the working schoolman. What is being done about French in Seattle? What is being done in the new physics course at M.I.T.? What does it look like? What does it smell like? What are the results? It is not enough for us to turn out these articles. In looking at them, you will see that they are not pieces of information; they are pieces about information. In a certain sense they act as an index. One article may report that if you go to Winnipeg, you will see a new kind of vocational program and be able to discuss it with the students and the teachers and, maybe, get some better ideas of a new way for vocational education. The article does not really explain much. It does say that the people there have what they think is a new way of doing something; but when you get there, you may actually find that it is not new to you at all.

I am suggesting that information is not only what you get in print. Information obviously is what you get in a personal visit, or a visit with a telephone video circuit, or by some other means. I am suggesting that we have not solved the problems of information retrieval and dissemination by applying the computer for bibliographical sources. Until we approach the whole subject of what information is, what communication is as a result of having the electric circuit, we cannot possibly begin to use our computers effectively.

Broadening the Spectrum

Alan M. Rees

THE REFERENCE PROCESS

The transaction at the reference desk is often viewed in simple terms. Library users ask questions, and reference librarians respond to the stimulus provided by the questioner. This is undoubtedly a most deceptive oversimplification. What is a "question" and what constitutes a satisfactory "answer"? Why do people need information, for what purposes, and under what conditions? Is the formulation of questions as presently conceived the best vehicle for the formalized representation of information needs? To what degree can an expressed want be equated with an underlying and inchoate information need? Is an intermediary such as a reference librarian really necessary for the identification and exploitation of information sources? What, in fact, is the fundamental nature of the reference process?

This term is used with deliberation since I wish to make a clear differentiation between reference *process*, reference *work*, reference *sources*, and reference *services*. The reference process incorporates the sum total of variables involved in the performance of reference work by an intermediary designated as reference

Alan M. Rees is Assistant Director for Research of the Center for Documentation and Communication Research and Associate Professor of Library Science, Western Reserve University. He has served as consultant to the National Institutes of Health and National Library of Medicine. Director of Training Program in Medical Librarianship and Health Information Systems, Western Reserve University. He is particularly interested in the coordination of information science and librarianship.

▶ [1]Based in part on work performed on NSF Contract C-423.

librarian. It includes both the psychology of the questioner and the environmental context within which the need for information is generated, together with the psychology of the reference librarian and the reference sources employed. Reference service is the formalized provision of information in diverse forms by a reference librarian, who is interposed between the questioner and available information sources. Reference work is the function performed by reference librarians in providing reference service. The perception on the part of the librarian of the need of the questioner is an important part of the reference process. The formalized representation of this need is the question, which may or may not be an adequate expression of the underlying information requirement.

The reference process, therefore, comprises a complex interaction among questioner, reference librarian, and information sources, involving not only the identification and manipulation of available bibliographic apparatus, but also the operation of psychological, sociological, and environmental variables which are imperfectly understood at the present time. A structuring of the reference process is shown in Figure 1.

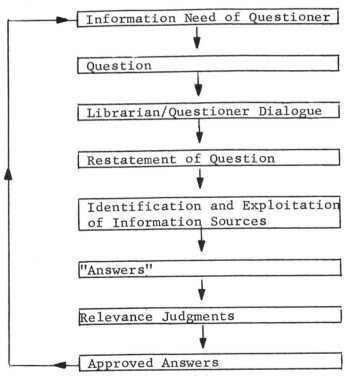

Figure 1. Operational structure of the reference process

Most forms of human activity generate a need for information. In scientific research, information is required for a variety of purposes: to provide stimulating material to spark a creative act, to design and execute experiments, to write papers, and so on. Cognizance of such needs results in the utilization of many communication channels, both formal and informal. Such utilization necessitates the formulation of questions. Considerable difficulty exists in this connection, since individuals often do not know precisely what they are seeking. The language of questions reflects the attempt to form and define concepts. In this manner, a well-defined and structured question might represent its own answer. This inability of questioners to formalize their information needs lies at the heart of the reference process. It is by no means confined to scientific and technological activity. "You see they will choke to death and die with the secret in them rather than tell you what they want."[2] This well-known phenomenon has been attributed to obstinacy, intransigence, absence of confidence in the librarian's ability to furnish specific information, and lack of facility with the English language. Such reasons do not take into account the complex motivations of library users. The exploration of possible patterns of question motivation in various environmental situations is a future task for experimental psychologists interested in cognitive processes.

Taking into consideration the recognized inability to read minds, how does the reference librarian operate? Basically, he plays the role of the questioner within his own perception of the question and the information-seeking environment. The reference librarian places himself within the frame of reference of the questioner and acts as his delegate. Relevance judgments are made within this perceived context. We know very little about the dynamics of the judgment process. Yet it is evident that reference librarians are programmed in the sense of the Manchurian Candidate to make relevance judgments on behalf of library users.

We at the Center for Documentation at Western Reserve University are doing some experimental work for the National Science Foundation in this connection. We are asking diverse types of individuals to make relevance judgments of documents within a simulated research environment in the field of diabetes. We wish to determine the comparative ability of various categories of persons to orientate themselves within a research project generating a need for information. We hope to reveal the consistency of relevance

---

[2]E. V. Wilcox, "Why Do We Have Librarians?" *Harvard Graduates' Magazine*, 30:477 (June, 1922); quoted in James I. Wyer, *Reference Work* (Chicago: American Library Association, 1930), p.100.

judgments among and between populations of judges, such as clini-
cians and experimenters within a medical school, residents, interns,
medical students, and medical librarians. How are M.D.'s programmed to make such judgments as compared with medical librarians? We are interested in determining the items of evidence,
textual and otherwise, which furnish cues on the basis of which
judgments are made.

REFERENCE SERVICES

Toward a Broadening of Information Sources

Traditionally, reference service has been based upon published
reference works, such as the "R" collections which stand in splen-
did array in our libraries, protected against the ravages of circulation. Great skill is exercised to deploy a limited budget in the
purchase of volumes predicted to be useful and versatile in reference work. Larger budgets for the purchase of such books, it is
often implied, would result in improved service. By and large,
however, librarians have not thought of reference sources in purely
local terms. In 1930 Wyer pointed out that "the conception of reference work which is limited to the resources of one library or
one city or even to books and print alone is out of date."[3] Six
years previously, in 1924, Learned suggested reference service
based upon regional resources.[4] The idea of pooling information
sources, of making the total inventory of all libraries available for
communal use, regardless of location, is not a new one. The outline of a national network of libraries was sketched as early as
1909, in Charles H. Gould's presidential address to the American
Library Association, in which he described a national library system with regional and reservoir libraries and specialized information service.[5]

The proposed design of a national library system and network
drafted recently by the System Development Corporation[6] and the

[3] James I. Wyer, *op. cit.*, p.12.
[4] William S. Learned, *The American Public Library and the Diffusion of
Knowledge* (New York: Harcourt, Brace, [c1924]), p.12.
[5] Charles H. Gould, "Coordination, or Method in Co-operation: Address
of the President, American Library Association, Bretton Woods Conference,
1909," *Library Journal*, 34:335-40 (Aug., 1909).
[6] U.S. Federal Council for Science and Technology, Committee on Scientific and Technical Information, *Recommendations for National Document
Handling Systems in Science and Technology* ([Washington, D.C.: U.S. Dept.

accompanying recommendations of the Committee on Scientific and Technical Information (COSATI) point toward acceptance on the part of the federal government of the task of ensuring that at least one accessible copy of each significant publication of the world's scientific and technical literature exists within the United States. If this were to be implemented, it would be possible for any library within the United States to have access to the total inventory of information services linked within the network. Very real problems exist, however, with respect to selection of "significant" items, production of union lists and subject descriptions, and transmission and display of information.

It is already possible to discern an emerging and loosely structured network. Although most reference requests can be, and will be, handled by means of local reference sources, there is little doubt that, in science and technology, the network concept is introducing a considerable change in reference service. The rapidly developing network of information services, based upon the centralized acquisition, processing, and publication programs of the National Library of Medicine, has had a discernible impact on the practice of reference work in medical libraries, which are becoming increasingly dependent on *Index Medicus,* the current catalog, and MEDLARS. The establishment of decentralized search stations of MEDLARS will result in further changes. It is most likely that the Library of Congress will provide in the foreseeable future a machine-searchable record which will facilitate the local performance of reference work. The cooperative cataloging and network linkage of the Harvard–Yale–Columbia medical school libraries represents a pooling of resources to provide real-time, on-line information retrieval.

Although no complete inventory of the holdings of all individual components of the nascent network exists, it is possible at the present time for a reference librarian with minimal local resources to tap a complex configuration of information sources: the national libraries (Congress, Medicine, and Agriculture); the National Referral Center for Science and Technology; document distribution agencies, such as the Defense Documentation Center, the Clearinghouse for Federal Scientific and Technical Information, and the Government Printing Office; the Science Information Exchange, for a listing of current research investigators and project descriptions; documentation searching services, such as the Automatic Science Citation Alert (ASCA) of the Institute for Scientific Information;

---

of Commerce, National Bureau of Standards, Institute for Applied Technology; distributed by Clearinghouse for Federal Scientific and Technical Information, Springfield, Va., 1965). 3v.

information-analysis centers, such as the one at Battelle and, in the biomedical area, at Columbia University's College of Physicians and Surgeons; libraries with specialized collections, such as the John Crerar Library; trade associations and professional societies which print and disseminate scientific and technical information.

The exploitation of such resources for reference purposes is hampered by the lack of knowledge on the part of reference librarians of the existence of many of these information sources, the absence of a complete inventory and accompanying subject descriptions, and the unavailability of adequate communication channels. Yet the attention presently being paid to the designing and integration of information transfer networks will most likely result in the ability to channel information requests between and among local, regional, and national information resources. Questions will be accepted and interpreted locally and will be switched, if they cannot be satisfied by means of parochial resources, to the most appropriate library or agency. The provision of teletypewriters, consoles, and the like will facilitate such information transfer.

Toward a Greater Depth of Reference Service

Traditionally, librarians have been concerned primarily with the furnishing of documents and sources of information. In recent years, special librarians, in particular, have been increasingly involved in the extensive provision of literature searches, abstracts, translations, bibliographies, and other information products. During the same period, several hundred information analysis centers have emerged, which are actively engaged in the production of state-of-the-art reviews, technical summaries and memoranda, annotated accession lists, bibliographies, newsletters, literature surveys, digests, monographs, critical tables, data sheets, and so on. These centers have emphasized the necessity of supplying critically selected, specific, and synthesized information derived from a carefully preselected store of documents and other sources. It has been alleged that the growth of information-analysis centers has been occasioned by the failure of librarians to provide such critical judgment.

Evidence can be produced to show that some special libraries have endeavored to match the spectrum of service provided by information analysis centers. There is, after all, no reason why libraries should not endeavor to offer information services based upon evaluation and critical judgment of the subject content of documents; but, in practice, this has proved most difficult to achieve. The principal obstacle lies in the different relationship which exists

between the librarian/user on the one hand and the information
center analyst/user on the other.

The environment of the information center and that of its users
intersect, whereas the library exists outside of the user environment. The staffs of these centers consist of scientists, engineers,
or information specialists, who are the technical peers of the users
and are often engaged for at least part of the time in scientific and
technical activity.[7] They therefore participate in the user environment, whereas the reference librarian is a passive and often remote
bystander. It is not just the lack of subject knowledge which inhibits
the reference librarian in science and technology, but rather
the denial of access and involvement in the world of the user. The
librarian's knowledge of the user is nearly always mediate, infer-
ential, indirect, and vicarious; it is never empirical. Whereas the
information center expert retains his identity as a chemist or as a
physicist and continues to function as such for at least part of the
time, the reference librarian, if he ever possessed such an identity,
quickly loses it, since no opportunity is afforded for its preservation.

There can be no doubt that the spectrum of reference service
must be broadened and that the information analysis center has
provided dimensions of information service which are at present
far in advance of that provided by most special libraries. It is
necessary to recognize that reference service involving the eval-
uating, integrating, and condensing of information requires increased subject knowledge on the part of reference librarians,
more insight into the motivation of questioners, and, above all, an
active involvement of the librarian in the research and development
process. Unless the reference librarian can penetrate into the intellectual and professional world of the scientist and engineer, his
capacity to render service is highly limited.

THE FUTURE

My remarks have been primarily concerned with the spectrum
of reference service in science and technology. In conclusion, I
would like to discuss one basic issue which cuts across all types
of libraries—is the reference librarian as an intermediary really
necessary? Is it possible for a user with an information need to
exploit library resources without the interposition of a mediator?

The design requirements of future libraries, as described

---

[7] G. S. Simpson, *Discussion of Functions of Information/Data Analysis
Center*; paper presented at the Institute of Data/Information Availability
(Washington, D.C.: American Univ., May, 1964). 20p.

several years ago by Don Swanson[8] and more recently at the
INTREX Conference[9] and in the stated objectives of EDUCOM,[10]
tend to exclude the reference librarian. It is anticipated that the
user will be seated at an input—output console which will enable
him to enter into communication with an automated catalog or other
bibliographic resources of a library or system of libraries. Swanson stresses the notion of programmed interrogation, with the user
reiterating his request on the basis of information displayed to him
on a cathode-ray tube. The direct linking of the user with the store
of information is seen as a real-time dialogue in which the search
question is specified and refined with the output displayed to him.

Such a notion is in direct contradiction to the traditional development of reference work, which has postulated the necessity for
an intermediary. In effect, the elimination of the reference librarian represents a return to the practice of "aid to the reader,"
which is the antecedent of modern reference work. From this
viewpoint, the librarian assists the user in operating the library
machinery; he does not perform this task on his behalf.

It is my belief that our limited understanding of the nature of
the reference librarian/user dialogue makes it most difficult to
formalize and program this process at the present time. It has yet
to be proved that an effective programmed dialogue can be maintained at the man-system interface. Would this necessarily be
more effective than that achieved by the reference librarian? Is it
justified to engineer expensive time-sharing systems on the assumption that an effective dialogue can be achieved? Do we really
understand the problem?

A great need for research is apparent, and unless this is undertaken, little more knowledge concerning the reference process
will exist in ten years' time than is available at present. It is de-
pressing to consider that insight into the factors involved in providing reference service has remained relatively static for more
than thirty years. It is becoming increasingly apparent that the
behavioral sciences have much to offer to librarianship by way of

---

[8]Don R. Swanson, "Design Requirements for a Future Library," in Conference on Libraries and Automation, *Libraries and Automation; Proceedings
of the Conference on Libraries and Automation held at Airlie Foundation,
Warrenton, Virginia, May 26-30, 1963* (Washington, D.C.: Library of Congress,
1964). p.11-21.

[9]Planning Conference on Information Transfer Experiments, Woods Hole,
Massachusetts, 1965, *INTREX: Report of a Planning Conference on Informa-
tion Transfer Experiments,* ed. by Carl F. J. Overhage and R. Joyce Harman
(Cambridge, Mass.: M.I.T. Pr. [1965]).

[10]*EDUCOM, Bulletin of the Interuniversity Communications Council,* v.1,
no.1 (Jan., 1966).

insight and research methodology, and since many of the problems underlying reference work are psychological, some fruitful research might be undertaken. If such research is not conducted within the library profession, it is likely that systems analysts and behavioral scientists will engineer information/reference systems independently, with the reference librarian perhaps eliminated or downgraded to the task of delivering documents or of handling routine factual-type questions.

Comment

Frances E. Henne

My remarks consist of three parts: an indication of some major areas of concern noted by at least two of the speakers; several related topics not touched upon or not fully discussed in the papers; and mention of the unsolved problems that the speakers have stressed. It is not my intent to present a summary of the four papers, but to select certain subjects that would seem to merit further elaboration or discussion by the speakers or by the conference participants. To this end, I raise several questions that have been prompted by the speakers' comments.

In the first category, four areas stressed by the speakers have been selected for mention. The first pertains to research. We are told that what research we have is old, and even that is scanty. In an excellent, detailed, and helpful way, the speakers specified many types of needed research. A next step, it would seem, would be that of casting their many suggestions into a form that would indicate the purposes for which the research would be conducted and that would give priority ratings to the various problems to be investigated. Miss Focke gave numerous suggestions about the types of research to be done first to meet the most immediate needs. (Another example can be cited in relation to the kinds of information that are urgently required to plan intelligently and soundly the reference, research, and resource centers in the different states and for the different regions.) What research should be done on a

Frances E. Henne, Professor of Library Service, Columbia University School of Library Service, is a member of the New York State Regents Advisory Council for Libraries and is Chairman of the Revision Committee of the School Library Standards.

local basis, on a state basis, on various kinds of regional bases, and on a national basis? What kinds of appraisals, investigations, and evaluations should librarians undertake independently, and what techniques will yield the most valid results for improving and strengthening services? Is quantitative research the answer to all problems? It would seem that, in one important area, the redefinition or the formulation of a contemporary philosophy of reference/information services must depend in large measure on judgments emanating from sound deliberations and wise contemplations.

What apparatus is needed for the findings of research to be synthesized and disseminated efficiently and economically? What procedures do we follow to plan a systematic program of inquiry and to proceed in an orderly way so that we do not merely amass miscellaneous information in pell-mell fashion or, in our great zeal to collect facts, do nothing more than beat down open doors?

The second area to be noted in this commentary relates to the statements or inferences made by our speakers to the effect that the reference librarian is apt to become obsolete unless... Unless what, specifically? And for what reasons? Again, is this a matter resulting from the prevailing confusion about the philosophy of reference services, or do other elements, not sufficiently recognized, affect the picture? One key element, mentioned by the speakers but not emphasized strongly enough in connection with the problems they have delineated, is the chronic understaffing to be found in our libraries. This widespread condition has probably created most of the inadequacies of library services. Circumstances cannot be improved in the way mentioned by two speakers, when they noted they would like to have adults in the community and students in the colleges know how to use the library independently because these competencies would save the time of the librarians and because libraries did not have enough staff to provide services otherwise. This theory has been an albatross in the school library field for years in those all too many situations where school administrators and others have felt that one of the primary reasons for making every young person master the *Readers' Guide* and other reference tools is that it ultimately saves the time of the librarian. Substandard conditions of staff have thus been continued over the years.

In all four talks, the theory was advanced that school, public, college, and university libraries should, if not must, make more use of methods employed in special libraries, by documentalists, and in the techniques of informational retrieval and automation. No one questions this recommendation, but it would be useful to have answers to two basic questions: what keeps us from doing this, and how can it be done quickly?

The final topic to be noted in this category was mentioned by two of the speakers and implied by a third: that we must pay as much attention to the "bread-and-butter" reference services, or to ordinary needs, as to the requirements of technology, science, or other subject specializations at advanced levels. Several questions deserve discussion. In the Great Society, with its emphasis on information, what plans are under way to develop a network of real information centers for the common man in the street? To Miss Focke's questions about what we need to know about consumers of library services, let us add another—what about the requirements and desires for information services of the nonconsumers? What are the implications of the library program proposed for Columbia City[1] for the ordinary needs of people everywhere? Will one of our goals be that of having learning rooms in as many homes as possible? What else can be done, and what else is being done, to meet these ordinary needs, and what are the implications for national planning?

The second category of the commentary notes briefly some "slighted" topics. No reference has been made to the need for a clarification of terminology. Lack of this definition may come from (or contribute to) the muddiness of the basic philosophy. Where, for example, do readers' services and advisory services overlap into reference/information services? Where are they kept separate, and why? In many libraries, as we know, all of these services are performed by the one or two librarians who constitute the professional staff. But, philosophically, what is our position on this point? One other query—has not the time come for considering whether "reference" is not an obsolete term and should be replaced by something more meaningful to those who are not librarians?

Surely, "newer" media in relation to reference/information services merit serious consideration, and perhaps the lack of discussion about this topic today is due to its inclusion in topics to be covered in later papers. Mr. Freiser made reference to the important work of Buckminster Fuller, and it is to be hoped that the implications for libraries emanating from his philosophies and activities will receive full treatment in forthcoming meetings. This hope applies also to such topics as closed-circuit television, wet carrels, programmed materials, 8mm sound loops, and the use of audio-visual materials in meeting reference requests of library patrons.

Another point not mentioned today, but perhaps will be tomorrow, concerns the environment of the learning situation, or the

---

[1]C. Walter Stone and others, *A Library Program for Columbia* ₁Maryland₁ (Pittsburgh, 1965).

environment in which the end product of reference/information service takes place. What kinds of environment, and what kinds of library facilities, are we providing to achieve optimum results for the library users? Content can be piped into the homes of Columbia City, and carrels are provided for one third or more of the student enrollment in some schools and colleges, but what else is evolving? For example, how effectively are we using the mechanically controlled banks of information that are being developed in school library facilities?

A vital point that has not been mentioned is the delicate question of copyright. Let mention of this word suffice in this commentary.

There is no reason why our speakers should discuss time lag, and I bring in this possibly academic question only because it is a perennial puzzlement. Many of the things we propose and discuss today we proposed and discussed thirty or more years ago, especially techniques relating to computers and automation. What keeps these speculations from full fruition? What can librarians do to facilitate effectively the implementation of technological and other developments in the reference/information program?

Now, finally, we come to those problems stressed or implied by the speakers but presented without benefit of suggested or immediate solutions. I return again to what seems to be a primary problem—the philosophy of reference/information services. It would seem that we have not honestly or realistically decided upon a philosophy concerning the nature and scope of these services. How much service do we provide for whom, when, where, and at what level?

This observation leads naturally to the second problem—the ever fascinating topic of library instruction (or any of its equivalent terms in current use). Mr. Freiser and many other librarians believe that the time spent by students in locating materials is usually wasted time; that finding materials in itself does not constitute an intellectual process; and that significant intellectual activity commences with the use of these materials. I subscribe to these beliefs. For the formal agencies of education, from preschool through postgraduate experiences, recommendations for library instruction can be evolved only with the cooperation of educators in the schools and colleges. This problem falls within the framework of education first, and only secondly within the framework of librarianship as it is commonly defined. Although all problems are far from being resolved at the present time, it can be stated with assurance that our philosophy of reference service and library instruction in elementary and secondary school libraries has had a marked change within the last ten years.

Mr. Rees cited some extremely significant problems confronting us today. Only two are referred to here. He stated that the provision of information services through computerized technology, which would reflect a critical judgment and evaluation of the content reported through such machinery, is possible but, so far, has been difficult to achieve. This critical problem of appraisal of content stored in machines, not only of quality but also of suitability, is a key one. The second observation deals with his comments about the problems involved in establishing truly effective communication in the various dialogues of reference/information services: between patron and librarian, between librarian and computer, and between patron and computer.

Let me summarize briefly other problems that have been touched upon: the nature of library services for functionally illiterate adults in this country and the implementation of library programs for them; the need for close communication between and among all groups who are creating plans for the provision of resources and the services to facilitate their use—not just librarians in all the different types of libraries, but also school administrators, media specialists, and others; the nature of professional education for the future reference/information librarians; and the evaluation of reference and information services.

Our speakers have ably described the trends and problems in the achievement of the great designs for reference/information services for all individuals in this country. It has been a pleasure to hear all four talks.

Systems of Reference/Information Service

Regional and State Systems   *John G. Lorenz*   **73**

The Library Kaleidoscope: National Plans
    and Planning   *Foster E. Mohrhardt*   **83**

Discussion   **93**

Regional and State Systems

John G. Lorenz

In the belief that I was invited to do this job more on the basis of my former position than on my present one, I have related most of my material to public library systems and to those developed under the Library Services Act program.

I have always felt that it was a fortunate coincidence that the ALA public library standards, with their heavy emphasis on the importance of interlibrary cooperation and the development of public library systems, were accepted and promulgated in 1956, the same year that the Library Services Act was passed. As a result, most of the state library agencies included the development of systems as one of their primary objectives in their state plans.

What was not fully appreciated at the time was the heavy investment it takes to develop even one good regional public library system up to the level of ALA standards. And with so many urgent needs, including the strengthening of the state library agencies themselves to do a leadership job and act as a statewide resource, most states were not in a position to make the necessary investments to develop strong library systems. I recall how unusual it was that, for more than three years, the Washington State Library was willing and able to put all of its available funds into developing the Columbia River Regional Library up to ALA standards; as far as I know, this is still one of the best regional systems developed under the Library Services Act.

Another problem, of course, was that the Library Services Act

John G. Lorenz is Deputy Librarian of Congress. After long experience in libraries at the municipal and state levels, Mr. Lorenz served from 1957 to 1965 in the Library Services Branch of the U.S. Office of Education, from 1958 on as Director of the branch, and finally as Director of the Division of Library Services and Educational Facilities.

was limited for the first seven years to assisting rural areas only. As a result, there was little incentive for urban libraries to lend themselves as regional systems centers. Still another problem was the lack of funds for construction of buildings which could serve as systems centers. Fortunately, both of these problems were eliminated in 1963 with the expansion of the Library Services Act to include urban as well as rural libraries, the addition of a construction program, and, most important, an increase in authorization from $7.5 million to $55 million.

So it can be said that American public libraries have made a heavy commitment to the concept of regional and statewide systems of libraries on the basis that such organization provides efficient and economical service conveniently available to all residents of an area; the actual implementation of the systems concept, however, has been very slow in developing. Reasons for the delay include: the shortage of funds facing all libraries; the lack of a broad understanding of systems operation; the fear of smaller libraries of loss of autonomy; and the fear of the larger libraries of excessive demands on their resources without adequate compensation.

One of the popular elements of regional and state library cooperative systems development is the acquisition of materials and their preparation for use. Centralized processing operations can serve each library individually by offering such services as book ordering, cataloging, classification, card duplication, central billing, and the like, without threat to autonomy.

Another component of systems operation that is equally appropriate to centralization is reference, research, and information services. Like centralized processing, such services can be offered to each participating library without arousing negative responses to the idea of total centralization of systems operation. Further, cooperative information systems emphasize the specific responsibilities of each participating unit, as well as the services of the central unit.

Typically, public library regional systems have two major aspects: (1) a central library with competent staff and adequate resources to provide a specified range and quality of information in the general area of public library reference work; and (2) a number of participating or member libraries providing a specified limited range of "ready reference" services and referring other inquiries to a central source. Most systems use TWX or WATS (Wider Area Telephone Service) for interlibrary communication and mail or delivery truck for interlibrary transportation.

However, many of them also have distinctive elements. In illustration, I shall briefly describe some of the systems developed under the federal grant program.

SAN JOAQUIN VALLEY INFORMATION SERVICE

This system was organized in 1959 in California to serve ten libraries in a six-county area from headquarters located in the Fresno County Free Library. The demonstration phase of the system under the state library development program was terminated in 1961 and, since then, the service has been maintained on a self-supporting basis. The service was initiated in response to an increasing need for more reference materials, particularly those of a specialized nature, and for additional trained reference librarians. Photocopy service and in-service training for participating libraries were important parts of the total project. A multilithed union list of directories was distributed to member libraries, branches, chambers of commerce, and other users throughout the area. During the demonstration phase of the service, 5000 reference and research questions were answered, more than 15,000 photocopied items were supplied to libraries and individuals, and the service sold itself to the region in terms of increased regional support.

WAUSAU, WISCONSIN, REGIONAL REFERENCE SYSTEM

This system, serving 318,990 people in eleven north-central Wisconsin counties, is based in Wausau, which has the largest public library in the area. The aims of the system are to strengthen reference resources of both the central and the participating libraries, to facilitate referral and interlibrary loans, and to offer continuous in-service training of reference librarians. The state library will evaluate the project as a guide to planning other centers. The project began as a federally financed demonstration under the Library Services Act in 1961. By 1965, most of its support was being provided locally. Training of local library staff was an important part of this project. During the demonstration period, thirty-three training workshops were held which helped to stimulate the 23,589 interlibrary loans that were transacted and probably improved their quality.

NORTH BAY COOPERATIVE LIBRARY SYSTEM

Fourteen independent city and county public libraries are now participating in the North Bay Cooperative Library System in California, serving more than a half-million people in a rapidly growing area. The system was established as a separate public agency under a Joint Exercise of Powers Agreement in May, 1964.

The system, known as NBC, has set up suggested standards for

city and county library extension service for branches (in terms of
hours open per week, size of book collection, and population to be
served), for stations, and for bookmobile service.

Of tremendous importance to the development of systemwide
service is the intra-system development of service contracts. The
merger of the Santa Rosa Public Library and the Sonoma County
Library, for example, represents significant progress in eliminat-
ing the expense of operating two libraries within a single community and will provide for county residents an increased number
of hours of service, improved branch service, and bookmobile
service to formerly unserved areas.

In 1965, system activities included: cooperative book evaluation through review meetings and publication of reviews; the placing
of a standing-order program for continuations; a more than 9 percent increase in production of the processing center; the facilitation
of areawide lending of materials by improving charging methods;
the use of funds for improving book stock, providing copying equipment and microfilm readers, and adding personnel to effect broader
reference service; the continuation of teletype, telephone, mail, and
truck delivery service to provide the connective links in the flow of
materials and information; and the provision of audio-visual equipment in every member library. This is one of the major systems
developed under the California state plan, and its success is based
on much hard work by the state agency and on leadership in the
system.

INDIANA COMMUNICATION SYSTEM

The Indiana State Library, thirty local public libraries, four
state university libraries, and three other academic or special
libraries are interconnected by TWX for the purpose of making
reference resources more widely available throughout the state.
Reference referrals, interlibrary loans, and other communications
are all handled by this network. Smaller libraries, not directly
participating, may make collect calls to the nearest member library to take advantage of the system. There are several other
statewide and regional communication systems with variations;
but, as far as I know, there has been no evaluation.

BIBLIOGRAPHICAL CENTER FOR RESEARCH,
ROCKY MOUNTAIN REGION, INC. (DENVER, COLORADO)

The Bibliographical Center for Research is a nonprofit Colorado corporation, established in 1935 to facilitate the location and
exchange of research materials among the libraries of the region.

It was founded because of the lack of research materials in the individual libraries of the region and is an outstanding example of cooperation among them. Some two hundred libraries in the region make use of its services and support its activities.

In 1965, five states participated in the Center with Library Services and Construction Act services plan funds. Colorado, Nebraska, Nevada, South Dakota, and Wyoming paid membership fees to the Center to enlarge their reference capabilities.

Colorado's 130 public libraries were able to call on the Center for interlibrary loan requests, and 1300 requests were processed in the first six months of 1965. Twenty-nine of the libraries used the Center for the first time. The most significant aspect of this project is the involvement of smaller and medium-sized libraries which previously had not used the Center because of the fees required.

The Nebraska Public Library Commission pays membership dues to the Center to enable the Commission to forward requests there from public libraries in the state. In Nevada and South Dakota, requests to the Center are made through the state libraries. Six public libraries in South Dakota have separate memberships in the Center. The Wyoming State Library clears requests for services to the Center from the county libraries.

In such a sparsely settled, generally low-economic-level area, there can be little doubt that this Center has improved the quality of reference service which would otherwise be available or, more likely, unavailable.

CONNECTICUT

Connecticut is in the initial stages of developing a statewide plan for regional reference services. It is expanding the service area of five metropolitan public libraries serving a population of more than 100,000 in Bridgeport, Hartford, New Haven, Stamford, and Waterbury. These libraries receive per capita grants to support coordinated reference and research services to any state resident. Each participating library provides telephone information by reference specialists, photo reproduction and microprint reading facilities, and special files and indexes of state and local data. Each library also maintains special collections and services for research laboratories, business and industrial firms, government agencies, and other community groups. The state has budgeted $664,522 for this project, of which $209,156 were federal funds under LSCA for each of the fiscal years 1965 and 1966.

So there has been considerable development of state and regional reference and information service's under the federal grant

program, some at a relatively simple level with minimum investment, and some quite complex and at considerable investment. The
evaluations that have been made have been superficial, but encouraging. For example, one of the earliest projects in South Carolina
under the rural Library Services Act was strengthening the reference resources of the state library and the rural public libraries.

SOUTH CAROLINA REFERENCE PROJECT

As a first step, a reference consultant, with good experience
both in reference work and in county library administration, was
employed to have direct supervision of the program. A reference
and interlibrary loan collection was established at state level to
serve all public libraries. Grants of $2500 for basic reference
materials and equipment were offered to county libraries which
served a completely rural population and which met all state-aid
requirements.

A conference was held at the state library to give librarians
from the nine counties receiving grants an opportunity to discuss
reference service and to examine reference materials and equipment. Since none of the libraries receiving the grants owned the
periodical files essential to reference service, the majority included microfilm readers in their orders for basic equipment.
With these readers, the libraries would be able to make use of the
periodical collection on microfilm being established by the State
Library Board as a part of the general reference and interlibrary
loan collection.

The state librarian's evaluation of the project after the first
two years is as follows:

Although the basic reference collections purchased with
the grants were not extensive they were sound and resulted
immediately in better service. The reference consultant,
through field visits, carefully prepared explanatory material,
and a series of news releases, brought home to local librarians the necessity for good reference service to meet the
needs of the people of the state. Impetus was given the improvement of reference service from all public libraries
through publicity given both state and local level projects.

The reference and interlibrary loan project has been the
outstanding success of the state plan in South Carolina. Every
library in the state is using the service and to an unexpected
extent. The goal set for the first year of operation was passed
in three months.... One of the most surprising developments
was the immediate use made of the new service by business

and industry. Since all requests must come through libraries,
the success of the program is increasing the prestige of the
local library and its use by the public for reference and information services. This in turn is affecting the financial support
of local service.[1]

This sounds very good, but we need evaluations in more depth
of some of these projects, particularly the more expensive and innovative ones. These should be in the nature of cost-effectiveness
studies, which are being applied more and more to federal government projects, particularly in the Defense Department. This is
why I was pleased to learn that the Council on Library Resources
has made a grant to the American Library Association to study
public library systems. This study will include a comparison of
the services and costs of each system with those in the service
area immediately prior to the establishment of the system,
looking toward developing a measure of efficiency of the system
concept.

I understand that the New York State Department of Education
is doing a study of New York State public library systems established under their federal and state grant programs in order to
measure the results of the investment in terms of service to users.

These observations bring us to the shape of things to come. I
would say that the New York Regional Reference and Research Library Program provides us with quite a good look. The program
would create a statewide network of academic, special, and public
libraries. The network would be administered at the state level by
a State Reference and Research Library Resources Board and at
the local level by councils representing the research and academic
libraries in the area served. State grants would help support the
network under a formula based on the number of students in institutions of higher education and on the number of professional persons in the state. The design of each system would vary according
to the area served. One area defined five fundamental characteristics for a successful regional system:

1. An organizational structure providing administration and coordination of both the regional and the statewide aspects of
   the program
2. Reciprocal loan privileges
3. Enriched library resources

---

[1] Estellene P. Walker, "Improving Reference Service," *Wilson Library
Bulletin,* 33:669-70, 677 (May, 1959).

4. A reference center in the largest public library and a research center in the largest academic library of the area
5. A quick and effective means of communication among libraries and a rapid delivery service.

The same area listed nine services judged to be of first importance in getting the system under way:

1. Union list of journals and serials
2. Special subject-collection finding list
3. Other union lists
4. Reciprocal stack privileges
5. Preparation of bibliographic lists
6. Literature searches
7. Coordinated acquisition
8. In-service training
9. Continuing research.[2]

Within the general concept of a statewide network of reference and research library systems for New York are a number of special adaptations for particular geographic or subject areas. One related proposal is for a statewide system of medical library cooperation and support to help meet the needs of medical education, medical research, and medical care. The proposal is based on contractual agreements between the state and the New York State Academy of Medicine and between the state and the New York Public Library. These contracts would establish the two participating libraries as "reservoir libraries" for science and medicine.

A geographic adaptation of the 3-R concept has been proposed for the New York City area. The major recommendations are: the establishment of a New York Library Service Authority; the construction of an undergraduate reference library at 42nd Street; and a program for widespread interlibrary use by graduate students, researchers, and faculty among the area's institutions of higher education.

Governor Rockefeller's budget message for the fiscal year 1967 includes a request for $500,000 to begin the implementation of the 3-R concept. Assistance may also be available under a new federal program, the State Technical Services Act of 1965 (P.L. 88-182). This program provides federal assistance to promote "wider diffusion and more effective application of science and technology in business, commerce and industry."

---

[2] The various New York plans are listed and summarized in New York (State) Library Extension Division, *New York's Plan for a Reference and Research Library Program* (Albany, 1963). 14p.

Despite the lack of state funds to assist 3-R development, several localities have been eager to get started. The New York State Board of Regents has issued one absolute charter and two provisional ones to Reference and Research Library Systems.

The New York Metropolitan Reference and Research Library Agency was chartered June 26, 1964. The Agency will undertake to implement some of the recommendations listed above, leading to the eventual coordination of research resources throughout the metropolitan area.

The Southeastern New York Library Resources Council, chartered April 23, 1965, represents different types of libraries in eight counties on both sides of the central Hudson River area. A forthcoming survey of its research-service potential will help establish a plan for rapid communication and interlibrary delivery for reference and research purposes over an extensive and mountainous area.

The North Country Reference and Reference Resources Council, chartered October 29, 1965, includes two public library systems and four colleges in seven counties. Service planning is now under way, along with a survey of present resources and future potential. I am sure we are all looking forward to the results of these regional systems after they are adequately funded.

There is no doubt about the interest in Washington in encouraging cooperation between libraries. As more federal legislation for libraries is passed and appropriations increase, more and more questions are heard as to whether libraries are making the best use of these resources. Congressmen ask at the hearings whether libraries are cooperating and sharing resources or whether they are duplicating or competing in the acquisition of the same materials. As a result, under Title II A of the Higher Education Act, which authorizes $50 million for grants for college and university library resources, it is provided that combinations of institutions can submit requests for special grants; and one of the specific criteria indicated for the evaluation of special grant proposals is evidence of cooperation in the use of resources.

Another straw in the wind is the new legislation now before Congress to extend and expand the Library Services and Construction Act. Several influential representatives, including Representatives Fogarty and Perkins, and about thirty-five senators, including Senators Hill and Javits, have introduced bills to create a new Title III which would provide for the establishment and maintenance of local, regional, state, or interstate cooperative networks of libraries. Interstate cooperation is defined as the establishment and operation of systems or networks of libraries, including state, school, college and university, public, and special libraries, working together to provide more effective and economical services to all library users. Such systems may be designed to serve a community, metropolitan area, region within a state, or statewide or multistate area.

The authorizations are $5 million for the first year, fiscal 1967; $7.5 million for the second; $10 million for the third; $12.5 million for the fourth; and $15 million for fiscal 1971. These funds should provide the initial investment to establish some effective library systems involving more than one type of library.

In summary, it is obvious that state and regional reference/ information system programs have improved service. It is also obvious that what has been done is only a beginning to what needs to be done. Edward Bernays, the public relations man, visited the Library of Congress last month and presented his personal papers to the Library. He described how research has always been the basis of his public relations work. He also said that he has long been interested in libraries. To him, they represent—considering their value—one of the most unused public resources available.

Why is this? We are still not producing in many cases what the user or potential user wants. We still do not have the research which is convincing enough to get the needed resources for doing the job that is wanted. As a result, many millions are being expended in developing information centers based on computer programs independent of libraries, in many cases with little research or measurement of cost-effectiveness. I would like to see one piece of research in which two similar libraries were given the same amount of money to improve reference service, one through investment in automation, and the other through improved conventional library service under good professional management, and then test the results in user satisfaction. I would also like to see another research project that would measure the cost-effectiveness of an independent information center, and one added to an existing research library and built on the established services of this library. At a recent meeting of the Science Information Council of the National Science Foundation, Ralph Shaw said that he had looked into the development of about thirty information centers and had found that in all cases they had had to create a library as part of their service. That may not be a nice, neat, well-rounded conclusion, but it is probably provocative, and that is where I'll stand pat.

The Library Kaleidoscope: National Plans and Planning

Foster E. Mohrhardt

When librarians learned that documentalists were rediscovering, recompiling, and renaming subject headings, they emitted a collective gasp of shock and dismay. There is a feeling in non-library circles today that descriptors, special vocabularies, and thesauri are recent inventions unrelated to conventional librarianship. Some science information workers regard them as the *only* devices for locating information.

Most librarians have responded with disbelief and, in some cases, reaction—a reaction that ignores the stimulation and new direction that can and must be given to subject headings if they are to meet changing demands and needs. Some librarians, however, early recognized that these so-called interlopers, the documentalists and science information specialists, were bringing a much-needed user reaction to librarianship. These specialists have also directed our attention toward the need for scientific inquiry applied to librarianship.

Too many of us have tried to remain aloof from these exciting and practical opportunities for change. Librarians who have co-operated with documentation colleagues in new projects have

Foster E. Mohrhardt is Director of the National Agricultural Library and First Vice-President, President-Elect of the American Library Association. He is a member of the Committee on Scientific and Cultural Information of the Federal Council for Science and Technology; a past president of the National Federation of Science Abstracting and Indexing Services; 1966 Chairman of the Association of Research Libraries; and a member of the Executive Committee of the International Association of Agricultural Librarians and Documentalists. He is Chairman of Section T, Information and Communication, of the American Association for the Advancement of Science, and recently headed the U.S. delegation representing the National Academy of Sciences at the International Federation for Documentation meeting in The Hague.

contributed an expertise that has enabled these activities to be based upon sound planning, long experience, and good library practice.

Now the documentalists, science information specialists, and other nonlibrarians are rediscovering library cooperation and the possibilities of broad subject-oriented and geographically designed nationwide systems.

During the past five years, the library shore line has been swept by wave after wave of national plans and national systems, affecting all or part of library service. It is significant that the most publicized and discussed systems were developed by non-librarians. Dr. Stafford L. Warren proposed a "National Library of Science" in 1964, and the Committee on Scientific and Technical Information issued its "Recommendations for National Document Handling Systems in Science and Technology" in November, 1965. These are the two most widely discussed plans, although they were preceded by the Baker Panel of 1958, the Crawford Task Force of 1962, and the Weinberg Panel of 1963. Common to them all is a lack of feeling or appreciation for the national cooperative efforts established and carried out by librarians during the present century. Dr. William Carlson, of the Oregon State University Library, reviewing an article, "The Changing Role of Libraries" by William Knox, provides a practical reminder:

> First, his title itself is a misnomer. The "role" of libraries is indeed changeless. It is, simply stated, to accumulate, house, and organize the world's knowledge, or segments of it, for ready and convenient use. This role is by the very nature of the library function unchanging. It is only the methodology and technology that has been changing, is changing, and under the impact of tremendous volume must continue to change and to take advantage of all possible technological advances which will help to keep the rising sea of knowledge navigable.[1]

Carlson then lists the following ongoing activities as indicative of library moves toward greater regional and national cooperation:

Author Union Catalog—Library of Congress
Regional union author catalogs and bibliographical centers
Union List of Serials
New Serial Titles

---

[1] William H. Carlson, "For a Better Perspective," *ALA Bulletin,* 60:11 (Jan., 1966), p.11.

Regional depositories
Interlibrary loans
Farmington Plan
Regional cooperative acquisition and use agreements

He concludes:

> It certainly does not hurt to admonish librarians, as Mr.
> Knox does, and to urge them to take seriously their "personal
> involvement and responsibility for guiding the evolution of a
> more effective and efficient national network of information
> systems for science and technology." This, however, should
> be done in the light of their clearly demonstrable record of
> exceptional effectiveness, over the years, in these very activ-
> ities.[2]

Since this is a library group, we can probably agree that librarians during the past century have recognized the need for national library services and have initiated, developed, and carried
out many of the components of a national system. With this agreement as our base, let us further recognize a fact highlighted by the
title of an article in *Missiles and Rockets,* "National Information
Program Impends." The article states: "What a national information system means is that every engineer and every scientist could
have at hand all releasable information contained in every major
library and research facility in the nation."[3] Your immediate reaction to this statement probably could be phrased: "This is just
what our bibliographic services, interlibrary loans, and similar
library activities have been providing," which is partly correct.
We do have a good base and a kind of system, but what now "impends" is a system that will be different in degree, intensity, and
formal structure. Of all workers in the information field, librarians should be least surprised that a national system impends and,
at the same time, should be most anxious for its achievement.

Even our largest and most specialized libraries have now recognized that "completeness of resources" is a chimera. We are
led toward national and subject-based systems, not by the attrac-
tion of centralization, but by quantitative and qualitative changes in
our media. The continuing increase in output of publications, the
complexity of languages, the varieties of interdisciplinary needs,
the multiplicity of originating bodies, and the cost increase in all

---

[2] *Ibid.*
[3] William S. Beller, "National Information Program Impends ...," *Missiles and Rockets,* 7:18 (Nov. 1, 1965).

library activities leave us with the urgency for increased and
better-structured cooperation.

We have a variety of choices: to wait for the evolution of library cooperation into an eventual system; to encourage the non-
librarians in their efforts toward developing a system for us; or
perhaps to work closely with these groups in formulating a commonly acceptable plan.

We may not be permitted the first choice, since there are too
many pressures and interests for immediate national systems.
The second possibility will always place us as an element of the
"information transfer process" or the "document-handling system."
In this context, let us not forget that the 1963 report, "Science,
Government, and Information," does not recognize library reference services in "the information transfer chain." Nor will you
find library reference work specified in the COSATI national plan.

I urge that we follow the third course, a cooperatively developed system, with the hope that librarians will seriously evaluate
the implications of "the information transfer chain" and the broad
meanings of a "document handling system." Then let us demand an
equal study of library techniques, traditions, and systems from our
counterparts—the national planners.

COSATI has made two notable contributions toward the formation of a national library system. It has sponsored the comprehensive study of national systems prepared by the System Development
Corporation. It has also issued the COSATI national plan. These
now provide librarians with a base for the National Library System.

Much attention was given in the COSATI deliberations to the
broad system concepts. Considered were the following points:

1. A "capping agency" or new government unit, with supervision
   and review authority
2. The establishment of libraries or agencies as "responsible
   agents" for a particular subject field
3. A new federal operating agency, maintaining and operating a
   facility including all documents
4. A special government-charted private corporation similar to
   COMSAT
5. A National Library Administration, similar to Point 3 but not
   built around existing units
6. The strengthening of existing government units.

I would like to add one more possibility—building on the
strength of the Library of Congress, the National Library of Medicine, and the National Agricultural Library and then using them as

the base for a system of national libraries, as well as a national library system. You may have more advanced and challenging suggestions. Make them known, since they are urgently needed. I can assure you that COSATI will welcome them.

Among the most effective of our present national systems and the most responsive to the need for new patterns of service are the subject-oriented library systems—notably, those in agriculture and medicine. Medicine will be used for our case study as representative of adaptability, imagination, and broad-gauge planning.

Emphasis upon the MEDLARS program has obscured the long-range plans of the National Library of Medicine for a national network. Yet the impact may have tremendous implications for all libraries. The basic proposals are:

The development of a national network of medical library services over the next ten years could include the following features:

1. A carefully developed plan for the United States providing an equality of library access for health workers in all States.
2. A system or series of cooperative agreements between the National Library of Medicine and resource libraries strategically located in relation to the smaller libraries to be assisted.
3. Federal support for the medical library network through the National Library of Medicine by means of deposits in microform of the National Library of Medicine journal holdings, and support for operating costs.
4. Local cooperative agreements between the resource libraries and dependent libraries, which would include the provision of photoduplication and telefacsimile services in lieu of the loan of materials.
5. The interconnection of the resource libraries with the National Library of Medicine and, in turn, with their complexes of local libraries through transmission links for the purpose of data transmission and telefacsimile communication.
6. The establishment in such resource libraries of MEDLARS search centers with tapes to be supplied by the National Library of Medicine.

The resource libraries would act cooperatively with the National Library of Medicine in sharing the national interlibrary loan load, and to this extent would establish a Federal-private partnership. Such arrangements would be additional to the responsibilities of these libraries to their own institutions.

The costs of meeting these interlibrary arrangements could logically be assumed by the Federal Government.[4]

An additional element, the further exploitation of resources at the local level, was summarized by Dr. Cummings:

> For the Library to index all of the world's currently published substantive biomedical literature in the depth required by specialized information centers seems impracticable. The Library intends to avoid the waste of unnecessary duplication by supplying specialized information centers with relevant bibliographies on magnetic tapes, with the hope that these centers will then analyze and refine the material to meet their particular requirements. Already the Library and several universities have made cooperative arrangements to test this concept.[5]

A further statement by Dr. Cummings assures us of his hope that national planning will consider tradition and maintain a sense of historical perspective:

> I look forward to the continued use of books and computers as an aid to man's memory and as an adjunct to his skills and talents. Let us not, however, fragment the unity of medicine by attempting to exploit these new modalities of information and communication technology without considering their effects upon the welfare of people, individually and collectively, and upon the purposes to which medical teaching, research, and practice are dedicated. Osler and Billings were men who knew how to combine the past with the present, and concern themselves with the frailties of humanity. Unless their perspectives are retained, the art of medicine may become a cool unfeeling science, much to the discomfort of the patient and the practitioner.[6]

A basic unit in the national medical system is MEDLARS. "The MEDLARS system was designed to meet two major requirements, the publication of comprehensive indexes to the medical

---

[4] U.S. President's Commission on Heart Disease, Cancer, and Stroke, *A National Program To Conquer Heart Disease, Cancer, and Stroke; Report to the President* (ₗWashington, D.C.₎, 1965), 2:397.

[5] Martin M. Cummings, "The Changing Character of the National Library of Medicine" (a speech presented in London, England, July 6, 1965).

[6] ——— "Books, Computers and Medicine" (a speech presented to the Osler Club, London, England, July 12, 1965).

literature in various subject specialties and the storage and retrieval of bibliographic data upon demand."[7]

Reports and evaluations of MEDLARS as a reference tool for
satellite libraries are given in the *Bulletin* of the Medical Library
Association for January, 1966. The experience of Dr. Frank B.
Rogers at the University of Colorado is of particular interest. He
stresses the difficulty of trying to compare personal (or traditional) and machine searches of bibliographic references. He
does, however, report one highly significant comparison. "If the
costs are equal, then we may discern one very important point—
the machine way is at least four times faster than the traditional
way, and, more important still, in the machine way the efforts of
the reference librarian go at least six times farther than in the
traditional way."[8]

Your immediate reaction as reference librarians may not be
quite so enthusiastic as that of the administrator. I accept this
new device as an additional tool to aid the reference librarian, but
in no way as a substitute for his professional guidance and help.

Although our services in agriculture are not as computerized
as those at NLM, we are moving into information center work. Our
center concept includes evaluation of publications by subject experts, inclusion of nonpublished information, and selective dissemination. As we move rapidly into an era of computer-aided
sharing of library resources, I feel certain that, within the next
decade, the multiple-access computer will be in general use by
research libraries. I would assume that possibly in ten years, instead of mailing tapes to libraries throughout the country, we will
probably have the computers electronically connected so that each
can tap the other's information. We will not have a common computer storing all the information but, among research libraries at
least, a commonly joined computer system.

Before I leave this topic of the national libraries, I would like
to quote from an article by Thomas P. Brockway in the March
Newsletter of the American Council of Learned Societies. Naturally, research people are greatly concerned about library problems, and in the article, Brockway goes back to the Carlson point
mentioned earlier—that librarians have already experimented with
many of the elements of a national system. After indicating what
librarians have done, Brockway says:

[7]Charles J. Austin, "The MEDLARS System," *Datamation,* 10:28-31
(Dec., 1964).
[8]Frank B. Rogers, "MEDLARS Operating Experience at the University
of Colorado," *Bulletin of the Medical Library Association,* 54:9 (Jan., 1966).

From these remarks it should be clear that librarians are
aware of the crises they face, whoever else is, and that cor-
rective action is being taken on various levels. However, it
is not at all certain that enough is being done, that what is being done piecemeal will eventually contribute to an effectively
functioning whole, or that the librarian's potential allies are
aware of the gravity of the problems they live with.

To offset the piecemeal approach prominent librarians
have stressed the need for a national library system or program, "integrated but not monolithic," whose shared resources in whatever form would continue to grow, but in
orderly fashion and with a minimum of duplicated effort and
cross-purpose. . . .

In recent months noteworthy progress has been made in
the direction both of a national library program and of more
federal support.

The Library of Congress is the obvious keystone in any
national library structure, but in the past the case for its
centrality has not convinced everyone. Some have objected
that it could never be a fully National Library because its
first obligation must be to Congress. Whether or not the
point is valid, the Library of Congress has appeared to be
incurably short of space, staff and funds. . . .

At the moment, however, the Library of Congress is
looking and acting like a National Library.[9]

Now that I have covered, in a very general way, this development of national plans, let me mention two major developments in
abstracting and indexing services which will directly affect the
structure of a national information system. In the past two decades, there has been a tremendous expansion of government-
supported and operated indexing and abstracting services. These
must be considered in any comprehensive plans.

During this same period, such major nongovernment services
as *Biological Abstracts* and *Chemical Abstracts* have expanded into
more and more new kinds of direct or personal services of the type
that were formerly provided by libraries. These trends are important to us all in our long-range plans, and we should be relating
them to our present work.

My comments on referral services must be brief, since I find
it difficult to evaluate activities such as those of the National
Referral Center for Science and Technology at the Library of

[9] Thomas P. Brockway, "Library Problems and the Scholar," *ACLS Newsletter,* 17:5-6 (Mar., 1966).

Congress. They have been likened to the yellow pages of the telephone book. Frankly, I do not understand just what a referral center provides that has not always been a part of any good library
reference service.

Dr. Launor Carter, after his experience in directing the SDC
study, stated:

> The growing sense of the urgency of this problem [infor-
> mation] is not created solely by the faults of the present sys-
> tem. Perhaps a more powerful stimulus is in the worldwide
> awakening to the realization that information is one of the
> most precious of national resources.[10]

I emphasize his reference to *worldwide* awakening, since a proposal has been presented by the International Council of Scientific
Unions for UNESCO to study the feasibility of a "world scientific
information system." The world proposal has one selling point
that was never brought forth in the national plans. It would lead
toward peace in addition to aiding scientific, technological, and
economic progress.

Those who have newly discovered communication are now
enamored of the great importance of oral communication. Some of
the extremists believe that oral communication is relatively far
more important than publication and the work of libraries in providing access to publications. Some claim that our leading scientists do not concern themselves with publications; they merely
telephone their peers when they need information. The oral-
communication advocates, however, fail to tell us how these top
scientists communicate graphs, charts, illustrations, and data by
phone. They also have never revealed how these experts telephone
their predecessors who have died.

Just a month ago, Dr. Glenn T. Seaborg, Chairman of the U.S.
Atomic Energy Commission, was asked to comment on his work
that led to the discovery of the element plutonium. In his remarks
he said:

> But in recalling the story of plutonium I should go back
> further—perhaps to 1936 when, as a graduate student, I spoke
> in the College of Chemistry weekly seminar as was required
> of each of us once a year. Since the fall of 1934, when I began
> my graduate work at Berkeley, I had been reading first the
> exciting papers by Fermi, Segre and co-workers from Rome
> and then the equally fascinating papers by Hahn, Meitner and
> Strassmann from Berlin. They were studying the interesting

---

[10] Launor Carter, "The National Information Problem . . . A Problem of
Abundance," *SDC Magazine*, 9:14 (Feb., 1966).

radioactivities which were produced when uranium was bombarded with neutrons and which they attributed to isotopes of transuranium elements. I remember how I devoured those early papers and how I considered myself something of a minor expert on those "transuranium elements." ... During the two years following my seminar talk in 1936 and before the discovery of fission, my interest in the neutron induced radioactivities in uranium continued unabated and, in fact, increased. I read and reread every article that was published on the subject.[11]

We will probably find thirty years from now—as it was in 1936 —that advances in humanities, social sciences, science, and technology will develop from the study of publications, oral communication, experimentation, and all the complex of intellectual processes. National systems, computerization, and mechanization are exciting tools, but the ultimate user will still be stimulated by "reading and rereading every article" in his specialty and by "devouring" the important publications.

---

[11] Glenn T. Seaborg, U.S. Atomic Energy Commission, *Press Release,* S-5-66 (Feb. 21, 1966).

Discussion

Adams: I appreciate Foster Mohrhardt's very flattering comments
on my institution and should like to amplify his information.
The NLM plan, as presented, is only a portion of a total plan
under development at the present time. We have an official
requirement to prepare a five-year program plan. There are
several elements in this developmental plan which relate to
the points made. One of the things not touched on, however, is
the need for a centralized research and development facility.
We believe that systems planning of this magnitude will require a research and development program to pretest operational components to be involved in the development and
improvement of the system. We would propose to construct
a centralized facility which would be available, not only to
ourselves, but also to those scientists you have been referring
to, in order to study communication problems in the medical
sciences in some depth.

    Another major element in our thinking is the way in which
the planning is related to the educational role of libraries, in
our instance, of medical libraries specifically. One of the
continuing criticisms which accounts for the development of
such high temperatures and such interest in planning in Washington is that the results of research and development sponsored by federal tax dollars are not being adequately applied
to the development of the national economy or, in our case, to
the improvement of the national health. As you may recall,
Mr. Humphrey, when he was a senator, spent some three or
four years investigating the roles of government agencies in
improving scientific and technical communication related to
the application of research results. In the health field, such

application is fundamentally an educational problem, a function of continuing education. Therefore, one of the primary objectives of this national planning would be to give the library units an active role in support of continuing education programs in all the health sciences. In this capacity, we would look to other media, as well as to books and journals. I think scientific libraries have not sufficiently developed the very fine work being done by public library systems in audio-visual media, to give you just one instance. As you know, there are universities concerned with computer-aided instruction. We would hope to introduce, to test, and to provide demonstrations of new communication modalities to supplement the book and journal resources of these libraries.

I have mentioned only a couple of points here, but I might add something that gives this some substance and reality. It is the passage this last fall of the Medical Library Assistance Act, which will authorize the expenditure of $115 million over the next five years to develop the medical libraries of the country. The Act, specifically touching on regional or, as we prefer to call them, resource libraries, foresees their development into a system. So there will be sizable, possibly not adequate, but sizable, funding available to give reality to this planning.

Dubester: I found Foster's remarks provocative and stimulating, and I want to make a few comments, not necessarily in a sequence paralleling his remarks. Foster and many of the other speakers have recurrently alluded to user satisfaction as a measure of library service. I think we want to move a little bit beyond the acceptance of truisms. User satisfaction is probably a questionable measure of library effectiveness. The people who use libraries judge their own satisfaction in terms of what they have been conditioned to expect from libraries, and they are not always in the best position to judge. All too often, the reference librarian who serves the user knows that, if he were the user, he would not have been satisfied with the service he got. As a matter of fact, a more rigorous criterion, which we are at the moment unable to do anything about, is the following. A scientist presumably uses a library to secure, or try to secure, information needed in his work. The question is: How does information or the availability of information affect the productivity, the capability, or the output of the scientist? In other words, what is the effect of the information on the work of the person who uses it? The information has nothing to do with his satisfaction. He may not be satisfied, but he may do a better job; or he may be very satisfied, but show no effects in the work itself.

I would like to offer a thought that relates to the vicarious dialogue between Knox and Carlson to which Foster Mohrhardt alluded. Knox talked about the changing role of libraries, whereas Carlson referred to the historic role which doesn't need to be changed. I was carried back to the time at the very outset of the automation survey at the Library of Congress conducted by a team of seven very competent specialists, not many of them traditionally involved with libraries. When they were faced with the notion that libraries are designed to store and organize information for ready and convenient access, they said: "Why have a team of people trying to automate a library in order to accomplish this?" They felt that there should be a library that would go out and give things to the user and do things for the user, that is, do more than libraries are doing today. The closest echo of what they thought the library ought to be doing is what Mr. Freiser described yesterday as going on in Toronto, where the library is aggressive and anticipates and serves the user with information. Convenient access, or even convenience, is all too often defined by the library and not by the user.

I have one final comment about the nature of systems. In this morning's session, in the afternoon session, and in tomorrow's session, we have been, and will be, talking about systems. It is interesting that throughout, as we develop various definitions, the one term that is an assumed term and that is not defined is the term "systems." I am sure that everyone who uses the term is using it in some different fashion, and there is really no communication here about what a system actually is. Let me suggest that one of the details Foster may have overlooked in describing the SDC report for COSATI on the national document handling system was that the report made explicit the assumptions about the requirements the system was going to have to satisfy. One of the assumptions, for example (you will correct me, Foster, if I misstate it), is that the federal government should assume a responsibility for the availability of at least one copy of every useful document in this country. But, on the basis of this assumption and some others, the rest of the system just followed.

The crucial question is this: What is the system supposed to accomplish? All too often, the focus of system concern is with means rather than goals: are we doing the modern thing? Is it more economical? Can we cooperate?

But we fail to get at the basic issue of why have a system
rather than something that is a nonsystem, or, to paraphrase
E. E. Cummings, what is an un-system? For example, a system is something organized to accomplish something, but unless you make explicit the requirements of the system, you
really have not yet begun to talk about what the system is.
And when we talk about national systems, what are the requirements?

Foster referred to abstracting and indexing systems.
Where the National Science Foundation supports such systems,
one of the greatest problems has been to get the various pertinent communities to make explicit what they want to accomplish, whom they are satisfying, how they want to satisfy them,
and what the benefits of these alternatives are. These are the
problems of developing systems, and systems must be viewed
in terms of these requirements.

Freiser: I am reminded by Foster Mohrhardt's remarks of what
appear to be the defensive attitudes of a number of us on two
terms: "documents" and "librarians." I cannot agree more
with Scott Adams when he says we need to do and think more
of, and certainly require additional study on, other information
modalities (I believe that is the term he used), other modes of
communication, not the least of which are video and tapping information at source. Also, I cannot agree more with Henry
Dubester in his discussion of the responsibility we have for the
effect of the information that we pass on. As I mentioned yesterday, we are irresponsible if all we do is act as middlemen—
a type of activity in which we do not even check the information
passed on. Here, again, I cannot emphasize too strongly the
responsibility that is increasingly ours, namely, education in
the broadest sense of that term. In the field of formal education in the elementary and secondary schools, educators themselves are realizing that one of the greatest educational forces
or environments of our students is information. It may very
well be possible that not only can we conceive of ourselves as
librarians being replaced by information specialists, but that
—as teachers see sources of information becoming more and
more a vital part of the child's educational environment—we
may even be replaced by teachers as well.

We are defensive about the term "librarians" in a sort of
competition with information people, but we are not really in
competition. We are all people who are concerned with education in the sense of receiving information which is vital to our
particular or individual concerns. Therefore, since all of us,
with our different professional backgrounds, are in the same

game, if we consider ourselves as separate from the people
who are doing vital work in education, or as separate from the
people who are doing vital work in mass communications, or
as separate from the so-called information specialists, I think
that we not only will go our separate ways, but that those ways
will constitute a downward course.

Adams: May I address a question to John Lorenz? As you know,
the State Technical Assistance Act of the last Congress has
been called by many people the "sleeper" of the legislative
session. This is an act, for the benefit of those who may not
be acquainted with it, which assigns to the Department of
Commerce a role in organizing the provision of technical information in support of industry in order to promote economic
growth and development in the states. When you were talking
about state library systems, I did not detect any developments
on the state fronts where implementation of this act in any way
relates to public library development. Do you know of any?

Lorenz: This act was passed in the last session of Congress, and
I believe the funding is very minimal for this particular year.
My understanding is that the Department of Commerce is just
beginning to receive the state plans. I have been trying to find
out what the plans provide, particularly in terms of what
agency will be designated at the state level to take responsibility for carrying out the program under the Technical Services Act. The impression I have is that in many states it
will be the land-grant university that will receive the funds
and lead the program in the state rather than a state library
agency. I think this is natural, since the whole focus of the
act is to help business and industry get the information they
need to improve their products. This has been the traditional
role of extension programs through land-grant universities. I
have been trying to alert the people in the libraries of land-
grant universities to the potentials of this program for their
services. But I understand that in quite a few states the program will be entirely divorced from any kind of library-
related group and may very well be placed in the state
department for economic development, for example.

　　While I am here, may I make one other comment? I think
it is very significant, in terms of a national system development, that at the time we are moving forward toward new
means of communication of information, the Congress of the
United States has moved back to take care of one of the basic
fundamentals in terms of acquiring and disseminating information about materials. I am referring specifically to Title
IIC of the Higher Education Act of 1965, which authorizes

appropriations to the Commissioner of Education for transfer
to the Library of Congress to acquire worldwide all materials
of scholarly interest and to catalog these materials promptly
and to disseminate this cataloging information to all libraries
interested in it. As you know, this program was promoted primarily by the Association of Research Libraries in cooperation with the Library of Congress and the Office of Education.
The latest information is that there is a very good chance that,
even in the supplemental appropriation for fiscal 1966 now going through Congress, at least $300,000 will be provided to
start the program. Under the program, the Library of Congress will be utilizing all of the national bibliographies of the
world which are useful in the prompt descriptive cataloging of
these materials. It will be using offices abroad to acquire the
materials which we have not been receiving. Under this system, we can catalog the materials promptly and get the information out to research libraries.

In nations where there are no national bibliographies
which would be useful to us, we are planning to establish offices of the Library of Congress to hire and train local staff
to catalog the materials on the spot and submit the information as rapidly as possible to the Library of Congress. We
will set up about five offices in Africa, three in Latin America, and two in Asia to get the program rolling. This is really
an exciting program. For the first time the means may be
available to acquire worldwide all the materials of scholarly
interest and concern, to catalog them promptly, and to disseminate information to the libraries needing it. I think this
is very significant in terms not only of national but also of international planning.

Rees: I have a few observations. It seems that the most significant point brought out today, certainly, is the fact that it is the
responsibility of the librarian to be concerned not only with
the tools and techniques for providing information but also
with what people do with the information once it is provided to
them. It was observed that we do not know enough about the
nature of the research process to be able to determine the
optimum form of information that could be presented to a
person to improve his research productivity as a chemist or
as a physicist. I think that we need to know a lot more about
this. In the same way, one cannot discuss "physicians" without defining their specialization, institutional setting, type of
practice, etc. Statements such as "two out of four doctors

prefer Anacin" are useless. Who are the four doctors, and how are they chosen?

This problem underlines the fact that librarians are going to have to be concerned with the whole range of social, psychological, and anthropological factors before they can know, for example, the answers to problems such as: to whom are we providing information, for what purpose, and what is the impact of this information on the users? The essential issue is this: does this mean that librarians will have to transform themselves into psychologists, sociologists, and anthropologists, or will it be possible for librarians just to dip into these areas and apply the methodologies and findings of these fields? In other words, where is this sociological, psychological, and anthropological research going to take place? I am very much encouraged that NLM is apparently going to get into this area. The role of the library in the total information transfer complex cannot be solved by librarians who sit around and say that they think that the optimum type of information service or product is this or that. We need a lot of the type of empirical research which I am afraid librarians are not able to conduct. It was not taught in our schools of library science; where is it going to be developed?

Dubester: In response to Mr. Rees's thought, I will say that at the National Science Foundation we have been intrigued with this problem and have spoken within the staff of trying to create a marriage between groups having different competence. I think that if librarians recognize the need for competence in the behavioral sciences and social sciences and try to develop it, it will be a very long time in coming. Their educational training programs are designed to make them librarians, not social or behavioral scientists. It is possible, however, to combine the skills; the problem is: how is it done? Our present approach is to try to fund some research centers that will have a sort of tripod structure. We want to have research centers in the area of information activities that will combine a research and a training function in an operational environment, where the work can dip into pools of different competence, and where the work will also be tested. We have made a grant to the Library Research Institute in California, and we are also conducting negotiations on proposals with other universities looking toward establishment of such research centers. We are also encouraged by the efforts of some groups like industrial engineers in a university making an analysis of the library in the university. The marriage of competence is gradually coming about. In some cases, we have received library proposals and have told the persons to go back and talk to the psychologists on the campus and come back with a proposal that marries the library and—in the case of the behavioral type of research—the psychological study. We are getting an encouraging response.

Rees: In all fairness, I would like to add that the National Science Foundation is supporting some research that we are doing at the moment in conjunction with the Western Reserve Department of Psychology. We need a considerable amount of this type of work in order to know for whom we are designing our library and retrieval systems.

Neuman: All of this reminds me of the remark of the chancellor at the University of Kansas at the dedication of the Eisenhower Library: "These must be fertilized with money and irrigated with perspiration."

Reynolds: I may cause a slight revolution here. Do we need any more money? Maybe we are not doing enough with what we have. Cooperation has been around for a few years before 1965, and regionalism, it has been explained, is hardly new. Is our problem, rather, a negative attitude on our part toward service?

Lorenz: I can quote one state librarian who said: "You can develop libraries with money and without money. As the result of experience, let me tell you it is easier with money."

Reference/Information Sources

Currently Available Tools—Their Adequacy
for Today's Needs   *Katharine G. Harris*   103

Development of Machine-generated Tools
                               Pauline A. Atherton   121

Comment   *Edwin B. Colburn*   134

Discussion   140

Currently Available Tools—Their Adequacy for Today's Needs

Katharine G. Harris

Modern civilization is faced with two explosion crises: that of population and that of information. Heads of state and church leaders are trying, through conferences and councils, to develop controls for the population explosion which threatens the world's food supply. No one, however, is trying to stop the explosion of knowledge. All we, as librarians, hope for is some means to organize this mass information before it inundates us and all who seek to use it.

Reference tools form the system of communication by which facts and ideas are recorded; they may take the form of encyclopedias, handbooks, journals, monographs, reports, government documents, and so forth. Functioning along with this communication system is a tracking system composed of finding tools, such as indexes, abstracts, and bibliographies, whose function is to record the existence of other publications. The efficiency with which these systems operate in any field of knowledge is a measure of the adequacy of the reference tools in that field.

Thelma Freides of the Wayne State University Library, in her preliminary draft, "Sources for Research in Political Science," points out that the body of literature and its tracking system consist

Katharine G. Harris, Director of Reference Services, Detroit Public Library, is a past president of the Michigan Library Association and of the ALA Reference Services Division. A frequent contributor to professional periodicals, she was a coeditor of the January, 1966, issue of *Library Trends* on "Library Service to Industry." In 1965, Miss Harris received the Isadore Gilbert Mudge citation for distinguished contributions to reference librarianship.

of comparable elements arranged in reverse order.[1] The accumulated knowledge of a subject is built from the specific to the general,
while the literature search proceeds in the opposite direction, from
the broad review of the field down through subject bibliographies to
a single book and finally to a journal report. The depth of the search
will determine the tools that are used.

Melvin Voigt, in his 1961 study, *Scientists' Approaches to Information,* pointed to the definite relationship between methods and
sources used to obtain information and the purposes for which that
information is sought. He noted that certain bibliographic tools are
better suited for current bibliography and others for the exhaustive
approach. He says, "... the premise on which many bibliographical
tools are published—that they should be all things to all men—should
be altered and ... more attention should be given to designing and
publishing reference tools intended for a specific purpose."[2] In
other words, should we train the user to use the tools that we have,
or should the tools be adapted to the user? These are points to
think about, I believe, in surveying our current reference materials.

In any consideration of the adequacy of the tools we have or of
future needs, we must first of all ask ourselves, "Who uses our
reference resources?" All of us, with the exception of the special
librarians, find that students generate the major part of our requests. Students and faculty are the first responsibility of elementary, secondary, college, and university libraries. In most public
libraries, large or small, the overflow of students from school and
college libraries is creating very heavy demands on resources. In
a survey made at the Detroit Public Library in 1962, it was found
that 60 percent of the patrons were students and that, of these, 62
percent were college students and 38 percent were elementary-
and high-school students. The percentage might be even higher if
the survey were taken today. Federal money, now being poured
into education at all levels, may result in a reverse in this trend.
However, demands created by new teaching methods, upgrading of
school courses, and increased school population will still exist.

The research worker, whether he be connected with industry
or with a university, requires reference tools of wide scope and
great efficiency. He is the unique responsibility of the special
library, if he is attached to industry, or of the university library,
if he is a staff member; but many of his needs may have to be met
by other libraries in the area as well.

―――――――――
    [1] Thelma Freides, "Sources for Research in Political Science; a Guide to
Basic Publication" (preliminary draft; Detroit:. Wayne State Univ. Library,
1965).
    [2] Melvin J. Voigt, *Scientists' Approaches to Information* ("ACRL Mono-
graph," No. 24 [Chicago: American Library Association, 1961]), p.74.

Business and industry, for day-to-day activities, quite aside from research, have increasing need for the most up-to-date tools. Statistics in every field, government regulations, foreign and domestic markets, corporation reports, pictures for advertising copy, and quotations for executives' speeches all have to be quickly available in today's competitive world. These needs may be met by the public, the special, or the college library, or by a combination of all three.

Last but not least as a group of library users are the community leaders, whose ability to find the information they need affects the life of every citizen, whether he ever goes inside a library or not. The minister, the teacher, the social worker, and the government official must have ready access to information about every facet of today's fast-changing world. Increased concern for social and economic problems—education, integration, urban renewal, the changing role of the church, and government programs for the culturally deprived—is creating demands for access to materials which will help answer these problems.

What kind of materials are being produced today to serve these constantly increasing demands? How adequate are they, and what trends do they point to for the future? In thinking of today's tools, we must recognize the basic aids that we so readily take for granted. In 1882, *Poole's Index to Periodical Literature* took the first long step in developing a tracking tool for the control of periodical literature. Its successor, *Readers' Guide,* begun in 1900, is indispensable to every student and librarian. Specialized periodical indexes followed in quick succession, from the *International Index* in 1907 to the *Business Periodicals Index* in 1958.

Current American publications came under control with the publication by the H. W. Wilson Company of the *United States Catalog; Books in Print 1899.* Succeeded by later editions up to 1928 and kept up to date by the *Cumulative Book Index,* it provides an accurate and almost complete record of American and imported English book production to the present date. Since 1948, *Books in Print* and its *Subject Index,* published by Bowker, have provided the record of currently available publications.

In the many years that I have been a practicing librarian, I have seen the development of the *U.S. Library of Congress Catalog* in all its forms; the reprinting of the *British Museum Catalog;* the production of several editions of the *Union List of Serials;* and the inauguration by the Library of Congress of the union list of *New Serial Titles.* All these and many more bibliographic tools and encyclopedic works we accept as our heritage. They are still our basic stock in trade.

However, in every field, the system of communication is being
enlarged by a constant stream of new materials—in some, such as
science and technology and the social sciences, to a greater degree
than in others, such as fine arts. In 1964 Margaret Knox Goggin
commented that new reference books each year will increase pro-
portionately with the increase in the total book production.[3] She
also noted that dictionaries, encyclopedias, and handbooks were the
most popular type of reference book being published and that bibliographies, union catalogs, and catalogs of special collections, such
as those represented by the G. K. Hall publications, show the most
increase.[4]

These facts seem to be confirmed by a listing of the most useful
recent reference books just received from the heads of the subject
départments at the Detroit Main Library. Titles in the first group
accounted for more than one third of the total, and bibliographies
and union catalogs were the largest single category listed. In other
words, the need for tracking tools that show what has been published
and where it is obtainable is coming to be increasingly recognized.
Therefore, in considering new tools and needs, it seems logical to
start with bibliography.

The adequacy of these tools and the skill with which librarians
use them will determine to a large degree the amount and quality
of information provided for our patrons. One has only to look at
the remarkable summary, "National Bibliographical Services and
Related Activities 1963-65," by Helen Dudenbostel Jones, in the
Fall and Winter, 1965, issues of *RQ*, to be impressed by the number
of these tools and the fields and forms which they cover. We are
fortunate to have such a summary available, for keeping aware of
all tools would surely tax the skill of any librarian.

In the field of general bibliography, only a few important developments will be mentioned. One monumental tool, which is
saving countless hours of searching time, is the quinquennial edition
for 1958-62 of the *National Union Catalog*, published in fifty-four
volumes in 1963-64. And, of course, just arrived on the scene is
the third edition of the *Union List of Serials* in five volumes, long
awaited and of tremendous value. Supported by the Council of
Library Resources and published by the H. W. Wilson Company, it
represents the cooperative effort of 956 libraries. It is expected
to be the last of its kind, for since December 31, 1949, *New Serial
Titles* has listed in its monthly issues and cumulations the serials
received by the Library of Congress and some 637 cooperating

---

[3] Margaret Knox Goggin and Lillian M. Seaberg, "The Publishing and Reviewing of Reference Books," *Library Trends*, 12:439 (Jan., 1964).

[4] *Ibid.*, p.441.

libraries. Subject listings are, of course, available in *New Serial Titles—Classed Subject Arrangement.*

Another aid in the periodical field is the *Standard Periodical Directory,* published by the Oxbridge Publishing Company, New York, in 1965 and updated by semiannual supplements. Listing more than 20,000 U.S. and Canadian periodicals, appearing regularly at least once every two years, it is proving a useful supplement to Ayer's and Ulrich's.

New activity in the great European national book catalogs should be noted. The British Museum began, in 1964, to issue annual additions to its *General Catalog of Printed Books.* The 1963 addition in five volumes includes some older imprints, as well as the current ones. No annuals for the years 1956-62 (the gap now existing between the photolithographic edition of the catalog and the present publications) are planned, but a decennial cumulation of additions for 1956-65 will eventually be published to complete the record.

The first five-year supplement to the *Catalogue General de Bibliothèque Nationale* has been announced. The *Catalogue General des Livres Imprimés,* 1960-64, will be issued in twelve folio volumes of about 1000 pages each, reproduced in offset. When completed, it will greatly facilitate the searching of French publications.

Keys to library collections are provided through directories such as the *Directory of Special Libraries and Information Centers,* published by Gale Research, and *Special Collections,* edited by Lee Ash and published by Bowker, both of which have new editions in preparation. A new Bowker publication called *Subject Collections in European Libraries,* edited by Richard C. Lewanski, has just been received. These directories are of help to the rare-book librarians, as is another new publication of Gale Research, the *Bookman's Price Index,* which is an annual index to prices of expensive books and periodicals offered in catalogs published in the previous year in the United States, England, and Western Europe. It supplements book-auction records and is proving particularly useful for periodicals.

The latest effort to inform libraries of books in advance of publication is *Forthcoming Books,* a bimonthly publication of Bowker which began with the January, 1966, issue. Designed to supplement *Publishers' Weekly* and *Books in Print,* it is intended to cover *all* books of all publishers for the five months ahead. It should prove useful in ordering and in identifying patrons' requests.

Now I would like to consider for a few minutes some of the tools and needs in special fields, starting with literature. Due to student demands, reference questions have increased faster in this field than in any other for many libraries. At the Detroit Public

Library, the greatest increase in reference questions has been in the Language and Literature Department, whose reference requests have gone up 417 percent in the last ten years, as compared to 67 percent for sociology and economics and 125 percent for technology and science. The Detroit public school libraries feel this same heavy demand and are never able to supply the needs for literary criticism and biography. The reference books in this field noted as being most useful are checklists of literary criticism; American and British explications of poetry and short stories; and literary handbooks. Mrs. Faith Murdock, Supervisor of Libraries for the Detroit Public Schools, notes the value of the Gale Research Company *Book Review Index* for current reviews and says, "Any tool that would make information on authors and criticism more easily available would be useful." The Chief of the Detroit Public Library Language and Literature Department, Evan Thompson, notes the need for an easy-to-use checklist of drama criticism; criticism of Continental novels; quotation books with emphasis on current quotations; a last-line index to poetry (long requested by reference librarians); and more concordances to authors' works, which now can be produced by data-processing methods.

Noted among the recent tools in the fields of art and music are rather conventional bibliographies, dictionaries, and directories, with the need expressed for more current directories of such people as costume and interior designers, sculptors, architects, and landscape architects. A new comprehensive architectural dictionary to replace Sturgis (1901) is badly needed, and more intensive indexing of photography and numismatic periodicals is suggested.

In the performing arts field, new bibliographic tools seem most important, such as: Vincent Duckles' *Music Reference and Research Materials* (1964); the *International Inventory of Musical Sources*, which has been under way for some time and covers the United States, Canada, Latin America, and Europe, and endeavors to locate music written prior to 1800; Edith B. Schnapper's *British Union Catalogue of Early Music Printed before the Year 1801*; the *British Catalogue of Music 1957-*; and the *British National Film Catalog 1963-*. The marked increase in publication of thematic indexes in the United States and Germany is noted by Kurtz Myers, Chief of the Music and Performing Arts Department of Detroit Public Library. He says, "This is a field in which computer analysis is becoming important, especially in creating indexes to the incipits of collections of chant and other liturgical works of early composers." He notes that pioneer work with this material has been carried on at Wayne State University, Harvard, and Princeton. Needed tools are: a comprehensive annual listing of music in print in the United States, along the lines of the *British National Catalogue*

of Music; a music encyclopedia written by American specialists
from an American viewpoint; and adequate reference tools to cope
with the program aspects of television and, to a lesser extent,
radio.

The most ambitious new project in the music field is the *International Repertory of Music Literature,* which is to be an abstracted,
computer-indexed bibliography of scholarly literature on music,
sponsored jointly by the International Musicological Society and the
International Association of Music Libraries. Its immediate and
specific goal is to control current periodical literature and, subsequently, current theses, books, festschriften, and annuals. The
American Council of Learned Societies has provided a grant-in-aid
to make a study of the procedures and techniques of the project as
a basis for an application to a foundation for financial support. It
again points to the need for a tracking tool.[5]

A number of different trends are apparent in the social sciences, in which I will include education, history and geography,
business and economics, and political science. In the field of education, guides to new types of material are in evidence, such as
Carl Hendershot's bibliography, *Programmed Learning and the
Education Media Index,* widely acclaimed as a breakthrough in
electric processing but disappointing in its organization for easy
accessibility. Developed with a subsidy of $500,000 from the U.S.
Office of Education, it lists 30,000 nonbook instructional materials.
The Commerce Clearing House *College and University Reporter*
acknowledges the importance of federal programs affecting education. In loose-leaf form, it affords up-to-date access to legislation
and includes a good topical index.

Needs noted in this field include a comprehensive up-to-date
encyclopedia of education to replace Monroe and an updating of the
Vocational Training Directory of the U.S. A plea is made for more
current statistics from the U.S. Office of Education and more comprehensive indexing than is provided by the *Education Index.* A
simpler and more convenient system of issuing the USOE documents
is also needed.

Recent reference books in the fields of history and geography
seem to have followed rather traditional patterns. One of the most
useful of these is the *Worldmark Encyclopedia of the Nations,* which
brings together in one place reliable and up-to-date information arranged for easy use. Also noted as filling needs are the *Glossary
of Geographical Terms,* edited by L. Dudley Stamp for the British
Association for the Advancement of Science, and the *Guide to the*

---

[5]Conference with Kurtz Myers, Chief of the Department of Music and the
Performing Arts, Detroit Public Library.

Study of the United States of America, issued by the U.S. Library
of Congress and particularly noteworthy for its annotated bibliography of 6500 entries.

Among tools noted as needed by Rae Rips, Chief of the History
and Travel Department of Detroit Public Library, are: an analytical
guide to books in European history; dictionaries of European and
Asiatic history of a quality and scope to match the *Dictionary of
American History;* revision of the Federal Writers' Project guides
for all the states; atlases in fields such as economic and social
areas; and an English-language dictionary of archaeology of the
quality of the *New Century Classical Handbook.*

New tools in the business field have been developing at a rapid
rate, all pointing to the need for up-to-date and accessible information about foreign and domestic business activities. There are
yearbooks and annuals such as Beerman's *Financial Year Book of
Europe,* covering 600 major commercial and industrial groups in
Britain and on the continent; the *Food Industry Yearbook,* giving
pertinent facts and a who's who of the largest industry in the United
States; and the *Gallatin Annual of International Business,* with its
concise and authoritative summaries about every country of commercial importance. New indexes are extremely important in this
field, such as *Accounting Articles,* a loose-leaf service produced
by the Commerce Clearing House; the Funk and Scott *Index of Corporations,* a weekly selective index of 369 business, financial, and
trade magazines and of key newspapers, such as the *Wall Street
Journal* and the *New York Times;* the monthly *Wall Street Journal
Index;* and last, but not least, the *Business Periodicals Index,*
which could be greatly aided by an author approach. Despite these
indexes, there are still a great number of trade journals and business periodicals which are not indexed anywhere. One of the unmet
needs is for more extensive periodical indexing in these fields.

Another need is for a comprehensive analytical index covering
not only periodicals and pamphlets but also books in the fields of
advertising, banking, real estate, insurance, and business administration. The *Accountants' Index,* published by the American Institute
of Certified Public Accountants, could be considered a model for this
type of coverage.

In the field of political science, dictionaries, directories, and
guides are prominent among the recent tools. Two important guides
are the *ABS Guide to Recent Publications in the Social and Behavioral
Sciences,* published by *The American Behavioral Scientist* and providing selective annotated references to periodical articles and
books, and Eloise ReQua's *The Developing Nations,* listing information from books, government documents, international organizations,
and periodicals.

The newest tool in this field is, of course, the Universal Reference System (URS), devised by Alfred de Grazia of New York University and administered by the staff of *The American Behavioral Scientist* in New York. It is an electronic reference system intended to provide scholars with high-speed access to research literature of the social and behavioral sciences. It is claimed that the URS can review thousands of research studies in minutes and print out descriptions of pertinent items.[6] The first bibliography to be produced is *A Codex* (computerized index) *of International Affairs,* containing 3000 citations and 50,000 references. Later volumes are to be on other aspects of political science, government, and public policy. Future series are planned in all fields of the human sciences. Although the coverage is very comprehensive, the complicated organization will discourage maximum use.

Whether or not this kind of tool is the answer, there is definitely a need for faster and more comprehensive indexing in the social science field than either the *Social Sciences and Humanities Index* or *PAIS* are providing. Better and simpler indexing of the publications of the United Nations and other international organizations is another unmet need.

There is no doubt that the collection of materials is ahead of the ability to organize and retrieve it. A trend toward abstracting in place of indexing is noted in the social sciences, as well as in science. Thelma Freides points out also that specialists are separating in the social sciences and are developing an isolation as a result of this specialization. She finds that, to counteract this tendency, there is a new trend toward reviews of the total literature which give state-of-the-art evaluations.

School libraries report not only the traditionally heavy use of background material for American and European history but also the need for more materials on the contemporary scene: on civil rights, urban problems, food and housing around the world, etc. *Readers' Guide,* the pamphlet file, and free or inexpensive government publications are among the best sources available at present.[7]

In psychology, the *Cumulated Subject Index to Psychological Abstracts, 1927-1960,* just published by G. K. Hall, promises to be a useful and time-saving key to abstracts in that field for libraries that can afford the $650. In the fields of religion and philosophy, new tools needed are a revision of Hastings' *Encyclopedia of Religion and Ethics* (1928), new encyclopedias of philosophy and psychology, and more comprehensive indexing of philosophy journals.

_____
[6] "The Universal Reference System," *Wilson Library Bulletin,* 39:826-27 (June, 1965).
[7] Conference with Mrs. Faith Murdock, Director, School Libraries, Detroit Board of Education, Feb. 10, 1966.

The growth in scientific and technical research and the resulting flood of materials in these fields are, of course, creating tremendous problems of bibliographic control. It has been stated that
75,000 scientific and technological periodicals alone are being published, in sixty-five different languages, and that more than 3000
abstract journals are trying to digest this material into monograph
form. Much of the scientific and technical literature appears in
technical reports, conference literature, and annual surveys.

New tools in the science-technology field seem to fall into two
main categories: (1) encyclopedias and handbooks, and (2) indexes
and abstracts for the control of information. In the first group is
the indispensable *McGraw-Hill Encyclopedia of Science and Technology,* useful from high school on for its basic information and
broad coverage; it has been supplemented by yearbooks since 1961.
The 1966 edition, just published, incorporates part of the material
from the supplements. Other important publications are: the *Harper Encyclopedia of Science,* useful for school assignments and the
general public; the *Encyclopedia of Engineering Materials and
Processes,* with short descriptive articles giving enough information to facilitate further study; the *Encyclopedia Directory of
Physics,* edited by J. Thewlis; and the monumental *Handbuch der
Physik,* with individual volumes on particular subjects, many articles in English, and bilingual indexes.

In no other field have the tracking tools developed to such a
degree as in the field of science and technology, and nowhere else
has the effect of automation been so keenly felt. One of the most
important of these tools is the *Government Wide Index,* February,
1965-, produced by the Clearing House for Federal Science and
Technical Information and consolidating the indexing of four government index publications: *Nuclear Science Abstracts, Scientific
and Technical Aerospace Reports, Technical Abstract Bulletins,*
and *U.S. Government Research and Development Reports. The
Guide to Information Sources in Space Science and Technology,* by
Bernard Fry and Foster Mohrhardt, is the first of a projected
series of guides to information sources in science and technology
which is to cover mining, agriculture, meteorology, biology, plastics, power, and so on. These guides should prove useful as clues
to sources of information. The second volume in this series, *The
Guide to Information Sources in Mining, Minerals, and Geosciences,*
edited by Stuart R. Kaplan, has just been received. Frances B.
Jenkins' *Science Reference Sources* (4th ed. 1965) gives comprehensive listing in this field. Although without annotations, it gives
references to available reviews. A new kind of tool is the *Science
Citation Index,* which indexes items cited in bibliographies of articles in current scientific publications. It is very expensive, costing
more than $1000, and has yet to prove its value for libraries.

Currently Available Tools
                                                                113

The computerized indexes and catalogs will be discussed in
another paper, so I will only mention the *Index Medicus;* the "Plastics Section" and the "Electrical Electronics Section" of the *Engineering Index,* which are two pilot studies preparatory to subdividing
the entire *Engineering Index;* and the new *Dictionary Catalog of the
National Agricultural Library, 1862-1965,* supplemented by the
monthly *National Agricultural Library Catalog.* One feature of the
computerized indexes is abstracts with abstract numbers, arranged
in a classified grouping with a subject index referring to the abstract
number. This is a departure from the familiar subject arrangement
in the more conventional indexes.

Robert Gibson, Librarian of the General Motors Research Laboratories Library, in commenting on machine-produced references,
says that it is not possible to obtain ready-made answers from the
machine for special library clientele. The staff still must make
the selection and evaluation. As he says, the machine can do the
"chop-chop" part of the reference work, thus relieving staff to do
the more constructive part. Mel Voigt feels that better guides to
the bibliographical and reference literature of scientific subjects
are needed; he notes also the need for indexes to review articles,
better indexes, and listing of bibliographies, especially those now
appearing on cards and in other nonbook forms.[8] He considers
that the greatest information problem of scientists is keeping up
with current developments and feels that it is more important to
develop tools for this than for the exhaustive approach.[9]

The reference librarian in the average library needs good
tools on the popular level for students and laymen, such as an index
to science-fair projects, to mathematics, and to popular magazines
in science and technology. An author approach to the *Applied Science and Technology Index* would be helpful. A good new technical
dictionary and a modern version of the old *Machinery's Encyclopedia* are needed. In the more specialized fields, we need a better
source for identifying conferences and symposia.

Robert Gibson, having had experience in both engineering and
scientific libraries, notes that engineers use foreign materials
much less than scientists, either because they are less able or because they are less willing to read foreign languages.[10] Therefore,
translations become of great importance in the engineering field.

The field of biography, widely used in school assignments and
providing important background material for all disciplines, seems

[8]Melvin J. Voigt, *op. cit.,* p.80.
[9]*Ibid.,* p.78.
[10]Conference with Robert Gibson, Librarian, General Motors Research
Laboratories Library, Feb. 16, 1966.

not to have produced any revolutionary new tools. The who's who listings in every field and country are proliferating. *Contemporary Authors,* a biobibliographical guide to current authors and their works, published by Gale Research, is an indispensable first source for anyone who has been published by a reputable firm in any field except science, technology, or medicine.

One great lack in biographical literature is adequate coverage for the Negro. A current collective who's who is needed, with a classified index by profession and occupation. Leaders of local prominence throughout the country are almost untouched in existing books and indexes. A retrospective collective biography of the American Negro is also needed, but the lack of such a volume probably does not affect reference work as seriously as does the lack of current information.

Another lack in the biography field is a current who's who of men and women in the sports world, including not only players but also managers, umpires, owners, and so on. Sports comprise one of the great industries of the country and should be better recognized in reference materials. Book indexing in this field is notably poor, and few of the encyclopedias are kept up to date. Increased coverage of periodicals dealing with specific sports, such as basketball, wrestling, and surfing, should be considered for *Readers' Guide* or some other index.

In selecting reference material in all fields, there are three factors of importance: the availability of adequate reviewing media, the cost of the material, and the availability of space. Reviewing media are probably less important for the selection of reference books in large public and university libraries than in smaller institutions. Libraries with large budgets do not have to be so selective. Most of the new books are received on automatic approval, where a decision can be made with the book in hand, or ordered from announcements in professional journals and circulars. The reputation of the publisher and author usually will be the determining factor. Later, reviews will be used to check for omissions, to pick up foreign titles, and to test judgments that have already been made.

The department heads at the Detroit Public Library are unanimous in feeling that reviews in the regular reviewing media are not recent enough to be of much help in the current selection of books. *Library Journal* reviews are the most current and are excellent for music, history, and technology. *Choice,* originally intended as a selection tool for college libraries is proving of great value to libraries of all types because of the critical excellence and currency of its reviews. The special lists which appear in *Choice* from time to time are very helpful. Examples are: "Bibliography

of Lists of Books in the Sciences and Social Sciences," including
the last five years only, in the May, 1964, issue and "Library Materials on Southeast Asia" in the February, 1966, issue.

Margaret Goggin commented in 1964 that the reviewing media
have not been able to keep abreast of publishing and that the time
lag continues to be a serious problem for guidance in selection.
She noted that the quality of the *Subscription Books Bulletin* reviews
remains the finest, but that the number of titles reviewed decreased
from eighty in 1934 to twenty in 1961, with a time lag of eight
months from the date of announcement in *Publishers' Weekly*.[11] In
1965 the same number of books (twenty) were reviewed, and the
time lag was equally long.

Other general lists are: Frances Cheney's "Current Reference
Books" in the *Wilson Library Bulletin,* particularly useful for
smaller libraries; the annual selected list of reference books in
the *Library Journal;* the semiannual list of rather scholarly reference books in *College and Research Libraries;* the *British Book
News,* with well-annotated and carefully selected notes; the U.S.
Library of Congress Information Bulletin, with valuable notes about
government publications and other specialized materials; and
Stechert-Hafner Book News.

Each field has its own scholarly journals, in which reviews by
experts are available if time is not a factor. In many cases, there
is no approach to these reviews except by searching each journal.
A comprehensive service is badly needed in the field of the social
sciences. In the business field, about half the periodicals that contain good reviews of business books are covered by the *Book Review
Index.* The *Book Review Digest* does not cover this field to any
extent. Accounting, marketing, personnel administration, and
banking have special periodicals containing good reviews.

In the field of science and technology, the same problems are
evident and perhaps even more serious. The *Technical Book Review
Index* and the *New York Public Library New Technical Books* are
both slow in their listings. A periodical, *Science Books: A Quarterly Review,* begun in 1965 and published by the American Association for the Advancement of Science, has so far proved of limited
value for our library. The reviews, intended for layman and student,
are rated for quality and purpose. *Sci Tech Book Profiles* and *Medical Book Profiles* are new Bowker publications that reproduce the
title page, contents, and index of forthcoming books and would be of
some help in forming judgments where it is not possible to see approval copies. Robert Runser, Chief of the Detroit Public Library
Technology and Science Department, said at a conference at Madison,

---

[11] Margaret Knox Goggin, *op. cit.,* p.448-49.

Wisconsin, last year, in talking of the need for a selection tool in science and technology, "A basic problem of such a tool is currency. Science and technology are eager subjects, so eager that we are frequently asked for materials before they are published, at least in book form. The success of any developed tool would be in direct ratio to the time lapse between the publication of the book and its evaluation."[12]

Reviewing media for school libraries present a different problem than they do for other libraries. Very often, the selection of books is made at a central point for a whole school system. The Detroit public school system relies heavily on the Detroit Public Library for the selection of its reference materials, as well as for its general collections. The supervisor checks the new books displayed each week for staff at the Detroit Public Library and orders from them. There seems to be a trend toward examination centers for school libraries to aid in book selection. Wayne County maintains one outside Detroit, and such centers are found in California and probably in other localities as well. Small towns not adjacent to a center, of course, have to depend on basic lists such as the supplements to the *Standard Catalog for High School Libraries* and the new *Junior High School Library Catalog*. The *Booklist* (including *Subscription Books Bulletin*), reviews in school journals, and lists in special teaching fields are other sources. The *AAAS Science Book List for Young Adults* (1964) and the *AAAS Science Book List for Children* (1963), both edited by Hilory Deason, give evaluations and grade levels in that field.

In the development of reference collections, cost must of necessity be a very important factor. Whether a library has a large or small budget, the increased production and increased cost of books are a real problem. In this connection, statistics for a few important fields are given in the table on page 117.

With the index of 100.0 based on the average price for the 1957-1959 period, the 1965 average price for these same categories, excluding paperbound books, textbooks, government documents, and encyclopedias, ranged from 134.5 for business and 149.0 for science to 208.0 for general literature.[13] Since, in these subjects, much of the book production has great value for reference use, it is obvious that, considering together the statistics of production and increased cost, book budgets would have had to increase phenomenally to have kept pace. There is little evidence that this is the case.

---

[12] Robert E. Runser, "Introduction of Tools for Selection of Science Materials," in Institute on Public Library Management, University of Wisconsin, *Proceedings of the Tenth Institute . . . , 1965* (Madison, Wis.: Division for Library Services, Department of Public Instruction, 1965), p.43-46.

[13] "Index of Prices of Hard Cover Books by Category, 1957-59 through 1965," *Publishers' Weekly,* 189:69 (Jan. 17, 1966).

Category	New Titles 1957	New Titles 1965	Percent of Increase
AMERICAN BOOK TITLE OUTPUT, 1957, 1965, WITH PERCENT OF INCREASE [14]			
Literature, General (incl. Poetry and Drama)	855	1941	127
Business	266	437	64
Sociology and Economics	416	2372	470
Science	697	1850	165
Technology	316	942	198

In the science and technical book fields, there are special
problems that are of concern to book publishers and to libraries,
whether they be public, university, or special. Curtis Benjamin, a
vice-president of McGraw-Hill Publishing Company, has discussed
some of these problems in *Special Libraries* for November, 1965,
and in the *ALA Bulletin* for January, 1965.[15] He predicts that, in
the next five to twenty years, the cost of advanced treatises, monographs, handbooks, symposia, and the like may become prohibitive.
He bases this prediction on what he calls the "twigging phenomenon"
—the fractionation of knowledge in technical fields. The tree of
knowledge, he says, grows larger but the twigs remain the same
size as they were twenty years ago. Therefore, the specialized
market has remained the same, while the production costs have
risen 100 percent. He attributes the rise in the production costs
to the lack of technical innovations for reducing the cost of setting
type and to the restrictive clause in the 1891 copyright law which
prevents manufacturers from taking advantage of lower production
costs abroad. In answer to this statement, the rather frightening
article in *Newsweek,* called "Good-by to Gutenberg,"[16] points to
new technological changes which may wipe out the publishing industry as it is known today. However, for the present, Mr. Benjamin's points are probably valid when he says that, due to photocopying, automated libraries, and the twigging phenomenon, the
market for specialized materials will become thinner, and the

---

[14] "American Book Title Output, 1965," *Publishers' Weekly,* 189:50 (Jan.
17, 1966); *American Library Annual and Book Trade Almanac, 1959* (New
York: Bowker, 1958), p.43.

[15] Curtis G. Benjamin, "Everything Is Not Coming Up Roses," *Special Libraries,* 56:637-41 (Nov., 1965); "The High Price of Technical Books," *ALA
Bulletin,* 59:61-64 (Jan., 1965).

[16] "Good-by to Gutenberg," *Newsweek,* 67:85-88 (Jan. 24, 1966).

publishers may have to produce 100 copies at $500 instead of runs
of 5000 copies at $10, which might well price the books out of the
reach of most libraries.

The role of the federal government as a producer of scientific
and technical information is of concern to the publishing industry
and could result in the curtailment of book production in these fields
before we all are ready for the new technology. Mr. Benjamin says,
"Perhaps this development is inevitable, but if private publishers
are excluded from participation in the production and dissemination
of government-sponsored works, then much harm will be done to
the total information industry."[17]

Whatever the reasons, it is apparent that many reference tools
are becoming prohibitively expensive. *Chemical Abstracts* was
dropped by the Detroit Public Library in 1961 when the annual subscription price jumped from $570 to $925. It has now reached
$1200. Even at this price, it has not been able to maintain up-to-
date abstracting, and we miss it very little as a current tool. The
Engineering Index card service, costing $1500, was dropped several
years ago, and we find the monthly *Index* with the new "Electrical
Electronics" and "Plastics" sections, at a cost of $445 per year,
sufficient.

Two other trends in the publication of reference books were
noted by Mrs. Goggin and should be mentioned here. One is the
growing production of reference books in paperback. She noted
that, in *Paperbound Books in Print* for October, 1963, 377 paper-
backs were classified as "reference."[18] In the issue for February,
1966, 650 titles were in this category. Publication in this format
has important implications for the small library budget but may
also make it possible for larger libraries to duplicate some reference materials more generously. The fact that some titles of
reference value are appearing only in paperback raises problems
of binding and preservation which I will not discuss here.

The other trend of importance, which is growing at a great
pace, is the reprinting of reference tools and periodicals. This is,
of course, a great boon to new libraries, and particularly to college
libraries, which are mushrooming all over the country. For the
established library, these fresh reprints raise certain budgetary
problems. How much money should be spent in replacing shabby
but usable volumes when there is so much new material to be purchased? I, personally, am not sure to what extent we should be
filling in gaps in our serial files as reprints become available,
since these materials may eventually be available on film or tape.

---

[17]Curtis G. Benjamin, *Special Libraries*, 56:641 (Nov., 1965).
[18]Margaret Knox Goggin, *op. cit.*, p.443.

This brings me to the last problem that I want to mention in connection with our reference tools. That is the consideration of space. The Detroit Public Library completed, in 1963, a $10.5 million addition to its Main Library, more than doubling the stack capacity of the original building. Today, the library is comfortably filled in most areas, but the technology and science storage area is already crowded. Serials, indexing and abstracting services, government publications, and the like are eating up space at an unbelievable rate.

George Mallinson of Western Michigan University, in the *Education Digest* in 1964, pointed to the fact that in the 1960's knowledge is said to be doubling every seven years. He says: "...if major universities acquire materials at the current rate, by 1970 their libraries will need five additional miles of shelving."[19] This seems to point to two conclusions. One is that much more material will have to become available and be accepted in microform, and the other is that areas of specialization will have to be more widely accepted by libraries of all types. It will not long be possible for any but the very largest libraries to acquire all the currently available reference tools. There will be neither money nor space for the duplication of specialized materials. Since Wayne State University Library and the Detroit Public Library started their Joint Acquisition Committee in 1957, about $50,000 worth of such material has been divided between the two libraries, thus making it possible to spread their resources. Small libraries will have to depend on larger libraries in their areas for many important reference materials, and provision must be made for areawide support of these reference centers through state or federal financing.

How adequate are the currently available tools for today's needs? It is hard to give an answer. Informational materials to extend our system of communication are being produced in great quantity; many of them are of fine quality, from the general encyclopedias to specialized materials in all fields. These and the tracking tools to make them available are appearing in all forms, from the conventional book form to microforms and tapes. The homemade index, on which librarians of the past spent so much of their time, has been almost entirely supplanted in the last ten years by published guides. Yet many tools that are being produced today are not as good as they should be. Editing is careless; binding is poor; so-called "new editions" have a minimum of revision; and indexes are lacking or poor. Hester Hoffman, editor of *The Reader's Adviser*, says, "Whether a reference book is easy or hard to

---

[19]George G. Mallinson, "Will Books Become Obsolete?" *Education Digest*, 30:44 (Nov., 1964).

use depends largely upon the index.... Good indexes are rare; and the poorer the index, the greater the skill that is required to make use of it."[20] We have a right to expect excellent indexes in reference tools, and automation should make it possible.

Librarians in all fields and all types of libraries have an uneasy feeling that the controls are not keeping up with the explosion of knowledge. The need is for tools of greater scope, depth, and currency than are available today, so that the librarian can better perform his role of providing what Stephen McCarthy and Raynard Swank call "an evaluative, selective and personalized kind of service." [21]

[20] Hester R. Hoffman, *The Reader's Adviser* (10th ed., rev. and enl.; New York: Bowker, 1964), p.61.

[21] Stephen A. McCarthy and Raynard C. Swank, quoted in Gordon Williams, "The Center for Research Libraries: Its New Organization and Programs," *Library Journal,* 90:2948 (July, 1965).

Further information for this article was obtained through conferences with Howard A. Sullivan and Mrs. Thelma Freides, Wayne State University Libraries, February 17, 1966, and from notes furnished by subject department chiefs at the Detroit Main Library.

Sci Tech Book Profiles and *Medical Book Profiles,* referred to on p.115, are no longer published.

Development of Machine-generated Tools

Pauline A. Atherton

At the outset, it might be well for me to define what I do and do not mean by "machine-generated reference tools." I intend to use the term *machine* very broadly to mean any form of data-processing equipment (sorter, collater, or computer, including computerized typesetting or printing equipment). The term "machine-generated tools" includes the finished printed products, such as books, journal articles, indexes, and abstract journals, generated by use of machines; it also refers to the information available in machine-readable form. I am not going to consider as machine-generated tools those products which are merely microforms or reductions of the physical documents. The important concept underlying the term as I use it is that the "information" which the reference tool contains is potentially more readily accessible because it is in machine-readable form. This provides a flexibility for the information beyond limited use within a hardbound reference book or a catalog drawer.

The types of machine-generated reference tools I would like to discuss cover all the tools which would be included in a beginning course in reference: library catalogs, national bibliographies, union lists of serials, abstract journals, dictionaries and encyclopedias, handbooks, manuals and directories, yearbooks and almanacs, bibliographical sources, subject bibliographies and indexes, geographical sources, and government documents. Examples of any

Pauline A. Atherton at the time of the conference was Associate Director, Documentation Research Project, American Institute of Physics. She remains a consultant at AIP, but is now an Associate Professor at the Syracuse University School of Library Science, teaching courses in Information Systems in Libraries and doing research in the same area.

one of these types which are machine-generated (either printed or
assembled) can be found. This fact of production may be unrecog-
nized by the librarian using the tool, and the publisher may not be
aware of it, either. The present physical production method for
generating the physical *form* of the tools we use is important but,
for the most part, out of our hands. For some time to come, most
of the tools used by librarians will be sold in codex form, but there
are trends and developments in utilizing the machine-readable information of these tools in other ways. I do not intend to go way
out and describe projected, but nonexistent, information systems
which may eventually replace present tools. The stress of my argument is on the utilization of information in new ways because of
its potential availability in new formats; otherwise, for example,
the tapes used for printing might be considered as waste products
by the printer, once the reference tool is printed. We, as buyers
and makers of reference tools, will have to experiment with ways
to use these by-products to best advantage.

Before discussing the potential of machine-generated reference
tools, I would like to mention certain basic requirements of reference librarians which should be kept in mind when discussing all
reference tools, especially those now machine-generated. I do not
feel enough stress has been put on these requirements as yet.

Don Swanson, in the February, 1966, issue of the *Bulletin of
the Atomic Scientists,* talked about improving communication
among scientists.[1] What he described as the basic requirement of
the customers of our services could just as easily be described as
a requirement of reference librarians—the *principle of least action.*
Swanson said, "The design of any *information service* should be
predicated on the assumption that its customers will *exert minimal
effort in order to receive its benefits.*" Reference librarians, to
provide adequate service and do their work well, also require (2)
easy access to information. Dorothy Sinclair has asked, "Can anything be done to reduce the number of hours we spend, often fruit-
lessly, in checking indexes?"[2] We also need (3) *frequent updating
of reference tools* which would greatly reduce the necessity of
performing long retrospective searches. We should be able to
place more reliance on facts and figures obtained in answer to current questions. Again, reference/information workers need (4) *less
duplication in the tools they purchase and use collectively,* and this
is where the greatest potential of machine-generated reference

---

[1] Don R. Swanson, "On Improving Communication among Scientists," *Bulletin of the Atomic Scientists,* 22:9 (Feb., 1966).

[2] Dorothy Sinclair, "Meanwhile Back at the Reference Desk," *RQ,* 5:11
(Fall, 1965).

tools lies, in my opinion. We need to reduce the redundancy factor in reference tools used.

A study by Roger Greer[3] showed that, from a random sample taken from the *National Union Catalog* of books published in the United States in 1961, *Publishers' Weekly—Book Publishing Record* covered about 85 percent; *Cumulative Book Index,* 91 percent; *PW, BPR,* and *CBI,* together, 95 percent, with 82 percent of the items duplicated four times. In a recent National Science Foundation-sponsored study of overlap between *Physics Abstracts* and *Nuclear Science Abstracts* (Greer and Atherton, 1966, unpublished), we found that there was an overlap of more than 50 percent in coverage of identical articles between these two abstracting journals. Excess duplication in reference tools surely violates the principle of least action.

Additions to this list of basic requirements could probably be suggested, but the requirements noted may be sufficient to highlight what reference-tool producers must keep in mind, collectively, if they intend to make a contribution toward the fulfillment of the principle of least action in libraries.

The different types of reference work must also be considered before we can properly determine the usefulness of the newer reference tools available as by-products of machine processing of information for publication or compilation. The following is a list of the more or less typical kinds of reference/information work, regardless of the type of library in which it is done: answering inquiries for facts and figures—sometimes called "ready or quick reference"; preparing bibliographies; assisting readers in use of library; making interlibrary loans; maintaining special indexing and abstracting services; providing translations; collecting information on library resources; cooperating with bibliographical centers; and producing union catalogs. All of this work could be aided by combined files of reference information in machine-readable form.

Besides the so-called "reference collection" of a library, the reference librarian usually consults many "reference tools" which are available in other parts of the library, such as card catalog, process information file, and serial record file; he also obtains information outside the library, from referral centers, other libraries, direct contact with specialists, and so on. Working with this mixed variety of tools, used separately rather than collectively, is one of the problems reference librarians and library users face

_____

[3] Roger C. Greer, "The Current United States National Book Bibliography: An Analysis of Coverage with Recommendations for Improvement" (unpublished Ph.D. dissertation, Rutgers—The State Univ., 1964).

daily. Perhaps only sporadically, but still in actuality, the typical reference librarian is already in tune to be "on-line" to the national "system", to use Verner Clapp's phrasing—if only such a system existed. What we seem to have is H. Dubester's "un-system." Against this backdrop of requirements, activities, and display of the variety of tools available, it would seem that the time is right for librarians to organize and effect the proper use of machine records developed during the generation of existing reference tools. If we did, we might have better tools and be able to bring about greater cooperation and coordination of regional and national reference library service at no increase in cost. The combination of information in the reference tools we want to use collectively could be used in a way we have not yet imagined or adequately planned for. As Don Swanson said to me a few days ago, the problem is one of organization, not of computerization. Computerization, or automation, is simply the means to effect better organization.

Joseph Becker, back in 1947, predicted what could be expected of library (and reference-tool) mechanization:

> From the flexible arrangement of the cards, bibliographies become readily available by subject, author, and title. In special libraries, where material on one subject is concentrated, the research possibilities of gathering, sorting, filing and printing information are almost limitless. Continuous machine interfiling permits keeping current with new entry additions.[4]

It has taken almost twenty years for the library profession (and some reference-book publishers) to recognize the potentialities of computers in processing information which, when recorded only once, can be useful for multiple purposes.

It seems to me that the trend in the use of computers to generate reference tools is to follow the principle of by-product data generation, beginning with actual preparation of manuscripts for publication. The H. W. Wilson Company and the Bowker Company have done some pioneer work in the combination, cumulation, and multiple use of records for producing reference tools, but their efforts are unfortunately limited. They do not adequately provide for the combination of data from *various* sources within and without their respective companies. If we agree that such is our objective, attaining it demands greater cooperation between librarians and reference-tool publishers to consolidate their efforts at mechanization and create compatible machine records.

---

[4] Joseph Becker (unpublished paper, Catholic University, 1947).

I would like to describe a research and development project of the American Institute of Physics (AIP) as an example of how a publisher can improve the situation. AIP publishes more than 30 percent of the world's physics research in journal form. This means that AIP has the potential capability for improving reference work in physics if all of its publications were available in machine-readable form. Imagine how easy it would be to use the information contained in these journals if it were possible to interrogate directly an information system made up of the original manuscripts and to search the indexing records provided as coded identification of each separate item in the machine text. The AIP project will provide computer programs for the production of: input for automatic type-setting (thereby helping the publisher); author and subject indexes (thereby helping readers and librarians); data for abstract journal preparation; citation index data; automatic search files for local information centers; and data for annual subject bibliographies and cumulative indexes, to mention only a few by-products. Many more reference tools can be generated with no additional keyboarding operations.

I said earlier that I would not dwell on nonexistent systems, and I meant it. Although the system I just described does not yet exist for AIP journals, the necessary technology for developing such a system is available, and we intend to do it within the next five years, beginning with manuscripts from only two journals. Accompanying this development will be the type of studies Alan Rees mentioned yesterday—psychological and environmental studies of users of physics information. We intend to study the variety of uses of this original data at places like Bell Telephone Laboratories, Massachusetts Institute of Technology, and American Society for Metals.

Many of the components of the system I have described are already in existence, behind the scenes, in many of the printshops producing the reference tools we use. For example, since January, 1966, *Psychological Abstracts* is available in print, as well as in machine-readable form, which is useful for by-product data generation. *Golden Book Encyclopedia* and the *McGraw-Hill Encyclopedia of Science and Technology* are also thus available but except for experiments in natural language searching, they have no great potential use. Several research journals are typeset and printed by computer. With slight modification, the machine record of several reference tools could be used beyond the automated printing process.

I do not have to itemize for this audience the number of library catalogs now available, in whole or in part, in machine-readable form. The numerous bibliographies with KWIC (Keyword-in-Context) indexes produced since H. P. Luhn demonstrated the method in 1958 is legion. Nor do I have to elaborate on *Index Medicus* and the backup service for mechanized retrieval searches of the medical literature, MEDLARS, at the National Library of Medicine.

Most of these machine-generated tools and services appear to have shortcomings, if the combinability and compatibility problems necessary to effect a system of these reference tools are taken into consideration. (The best summary of these shortcomings, as well as a discussion of the strong points of the KWIC indexes and other machine-generated tools, can be found in Mary Elizabeth Stevens' *Automatic Indexing: A State of the Art Report.* [5]

For publishers, as well as for librarians and information workers, there are many good reasons why reference tools such as dictionaries, encyclopedias, handbooks, almanacs, and bibliographies should be produced with the aid of machines which make it possible to:

1. Reduce the time lapse between a ready manuscript and time of publication
2. Increase efficiency in production techniques, i.e., reduce costs of preparation and permit complete flexibility (different type sizes and legibility insured if coded for automatic typesetting in a Photon, Linofilm, or similar photocomposing machine) of various tools in any desired format using the same data
3. Accommodate additional or by-product services or a greater variety of services than could otherwise be obtained
4. Facilitate cumulations and cooperative services
5. Attain continuous bibliographic control, as well as compilation capability, thereby making updating and revision easier
6. Provide for easy transmission of data to and from various places
7. Avoid duplication in sources normally used separately, now easily combinable.

If we compare this list with the requirements, librarians and reference-tool publishers appear to have common objectives. Chemical Abstracts Service, Engineering Index, American Petroleum Institute, and Biological Sciences Information Services have all increased their flexibility in providing additional services and

---

[5] Mary Elizabeth Stevens, *Automatic Indexing: A State of the Art Report* (National Bureau of Standards, 1965, Monograph 91 [Washington, D.C.: Govt. Print. Off., 1965]).

have improved their present abstract journal and indexing operations by using machines for part of the work involved. In government agencies, here and abroad, there is a strong trend toward machine-generated reference tools. Atomic Energy Commission, the National Aeronautics and Space Administration, the National Library of Medicine, and even the Library of Congress beginning this fall will have part of their bibliographic reference tools on magnetic tape, and experiments in a variety of libraries throughout the country will determine the usefulness of data in this form for various purposes.

Quite obviously a great deal has happened in the last twenty years in relation to machine-generated tools for reference work, but I have had to conclude that there has been no concerted effort on the part of any group to be wholly or even partly in tune with anyone else in producing compatible tools, easily combinable for reference work. It is as though we were witnessing a rerun of an old movie covering early railroad history. This analogy will continue along the lines Miss Allen mentioned yesterday, converting our freight trains of reference service to express trains. In the early days, everyone built railroad tracks and equipment of a different gauge. Engines and trains literally could not be switched from one railroad's tracks to those of another. The east-west railroad connection was quite a feat. Today, the tapes of one library's catalog are not easily combined with those of another. The serials list of one library or a group of libraries cannot be combined with the records of any of the abstracting journals, and there has been little done to effect a combination of library catalogs and biographical directories, and so on. We still have a long way to go, and possibly only some of us are on the same gauge track.

We are now getting used to the idea of magnetic-tape libraries of legal statutes and other legal records and of computer-generated concordances (first of St. Thomas Aquinas' work in 1949, then of the Dead Sea Scrolls, Matthew Arnold's poetry, and Anglo-Saxon poetic records). Automated bibliographies of the type mentioned in the February 24, 1966, issue of the *U.S. Library of Congress Information Bulletin*[6] could be the kind of tool used in machine-readable form in several libraries. I refer here to the *Deutsche Bibliographie,* which appears weekly, contains information similar to *Publishers' Weekly,* and has an index of publishers and a combined author and keyword index automatically prepared and cumulated on a monthly, quarterly, semiannual, and five-year basis. The day may soon come when all national bibliographies are available in

---

[6] "News in the Library World—Automated Bibliography," *U.S. Library of Congress Information Bulletin,* 25:111 (Feb. 24, 1966).

machine-readable form and in a computer store, where they can be used on a local, regional, or national basis, as we now use the *National Union Catalog*. Before this day is upon us, perhaps we should take stock of the possible effects and implications of these new tools and of their potential for new approaches to reference/information work.

Jesse Shera has said: "The potentialities of automation can free the reference librarian from the popular concept of a mechanical stack-boy...and permit the librarian to rethink the entire reference procedure...." Later, he commented on the opportunity automation affords "to analyze the reference process and re-define reference service."[7] Helen Focke mentioned the need to analyze reference questions. This is a natural by-product when we use machine-generated tools, e.g., the MIT/TIP weekly monitor record. The potential may be there, but, unfortunately, the System Development Corporation research team, which completed the report on a national document-handling system for the Committee on Scientific and Technical Information last year, could not report much evidence that librarians at present were looking beyond their immediate tasks toward a larger concept of services, based on the advances in library automation. They saw little evidence of great strides in expanded reference tools and retrieval mechanisms based on new technological developments. They felt that a "prescriptive" rather than an "adaptive" philosophy toward information-system automation was predominant at this time. This means that the computer, though used by the librarian, is regarded primarily as an aid in his work and only indirectly as an aid to the user. SDC also reported that capabilities for new applications were going untapped. (Parenthetically, I can say that many publishers of reference tools consider the computer an aid in the printing process rather than an aid to the ultimate user. Only a few farsighted publishers have looked beyond this initial operation in the long process of information transfer, which they originally initiate by the publication of information.)

In fact, the SDC team painted a very black picture:

Unless someone with unusual foresight and influence establishes workable standardization, the history of library coordination as a mechanizable system complex, may be as turbulent as the history of higher-order computer languages has been. Unfortunately, the rush of library automation efforts could be so rapid that each installation, preoccupied with attaining its own internal efficiency, might not notice the incompatibilities of its formats,

---

[7] Jesse Shera, "Automation and the Reference Librarian," *RQ*, 3:4 (July, 1964).

codes, etc., with those of other libraries unless strong efforts
—such as those that a capping agency could exert—are made to
coordinate these aspects of library automation.[8]

The future development of machine-generated reference tools
is bright, but there are storm clouds on the horizon. The possible
effect of present-day developments may be greater duplication of
effort and greater incompatibility. The requirement for positive
action awaits agreement in standardizing machine-readable data
and the creation of an atmosphere of cooperation among librarians,
between publishers and librarians, and between librarians and
users. Librarians and reference-tool publishers will have to strive
toward a common technological solution of some of their problems
and make an effort to avoid the duplication in services and collections of information we now have. A true "system"—an organized
whole—could be effected, but a whole new field of automatic
"switching centers" in the total information system will have to be
established. We may get the wherewithal for this from Title III,
but it will not work well if the right people do not get together.
It would appear that I am asking for the impossible when I ask
reference librarians, reference-tool publishers, and computer
technologists to cooperate, but we obviously have problems in
common. We should be able to work together toward acceptable
solutions. At least three of the areas of responsibility of the ALA
Reference Services Division, as stated in the Division's By-Laws
and discussed in an article by Frances Neel Cheney, offer some
guidelines for the librarian's role. They are:

> Conduct and sponsorship of activities and projects in ref-
> erence services.
> Synthesis of reference activities . . . in the various types
> of libraries so as to produce a unified professional concept of
> the reference function.
> Evaluation, selection, and interpretation of reference
> materials.[9]

---

[8] U.S. Federal Council for Science and Technology, Committee on Scientific and Technical Information, *Recommendations for National Document
Handling Systems in Science and Technology* ([Washington, D.C.: U.S. Dept. of
Commerce, National Bureau of Standards, Institute for Applied Technology;
distributed by Clearinghouse for Federal Scientific and Technical Information,
Springfield, Va.], 1965), Appendix A, 2:11-6.
[9] Frances Neel Cheney, "The Reference Services Division: A Look Before and After," *RQ*, 4:3-6,16 (Nov., 1964).

In some circles, I know there is inertia or reticence to consider new approaches to old problems because individuals feel that these approaches may be less than adequate for problems in their *own* libraries or publishing houses. It is very illuminating to present these dissenters with the evidence in the study cited earlier which documents the enormous duplication in our present national bibliographic tools; with Ann Painter's study on the inconsistency found among human indexers; and with the present lack of standards for measuring quality in existing systems. When we read daily of the new techniques for conveying information, of efforts of an M.I.T. Intrex research team to grapple with problems of developing a nationwide computer network that will make every bit of knowledge instantly available, of Radcliffe students using a computer by means of a teletypewriter in their dormitory basements while doing the laundry or drying their hair—when we read all this, we cannot continue to hide behind our own reference desks, surrounded by our own reference resources. Librarians will have to consider the impact of all these techniques on their day-to-day work, on their ready-reference questions and on their bibliographic searches.

The *Newsweek* article referred to by Miss Harris, "Good-by to Gutenberg,"[10] asked, "Who is killing Gutenberg?" It might have asked, "Who is killing Gutenberg and Marion the librarian?" The answer in the article was: rising costs, multiplying knowledge, *new techniques for conveying information,* and an exploding population. Whether you are a reference librarian in an academic institution, in a public library, or in a special library, whether you are a dictionary publisher or an index publisher, you cannot fail to admit that these are the reasons for your constant awareness of the pressure of time, of the limitation on manpower, and of the poverty of the tools and services you provide.

It may be that the users of our tools and libraries may solve their problems in their own way, and we may not be called upon to help. If that happens, *our* library problems may go unsolved. Don Swanson suggests that future systems must provide for more digestion, summary, and packing down of knowledge, which will permit scientists and others to progress without foundering in the backlog of published information. He states categorically:

> Present libraries and information systems wait to be used. A future information system, however, should seek out its customers....we infer that future systems will provide decentralized service points and selective, direct, and continuous distribution of information to customers. Service in response

---

[10] "Good-by to Gutenberg," *Newsweek,* 67:85 (Jan. 24, 1966).

to standing requests should be maximized, so that customer
initiative can be minimized. [11]

He implies that, if future information services do not perform these
functions, they will continue to be performed in the informal and
most helpful (as well as expensive) ways in which they are performed today: the invisible college, preprint exchange groups, etc.
    New information services, with libraries in focus and in tune
with information and data-analysis centers, are on the horizon
along with the storm clouds I mentioned earlier. The Technical
Information Project within the M.I.T. library complex, the Stanford
University Library plans for a computerized book catalog with remote access stations at places other than the library, and the data-
analysis centers and library complex at Oak Ridge National Labo-
ratory are examples of future relationships. But the trends are not
positively in this direction; some effort on the part of catalogers
and reference librarians, working closely with reference-tool publishers and information users, will be necessary.
    A major shift in outlook is necessary before reference-book
publishers and librarians will begin to see the need for adopting
the principle of by-product data generation within their own operations. We need to try some new approaches; e.g., we need to
learn from someone's efforts to combine such things as the Library
of Congress catalog entries with the tape used to produce, say, the
Dictionary of American Biography; the tape for *American Men of
Science* with *Chemical Abstracts;* the special bibliographies in
linguistics with the holdings of large libraries such as Harvard,
Yale and Newberry; or the *Readers' Guide* with the *Union List of
Serials* in a school/public library regional center. The computers
we use may need to have a little more advanced storage capacity
and speedier listing and list-searching processes if they are to do
these things, but breakthroughs and announcements of such technological improvements have already been made. What we desperately
need are more librarians who are willing to learn programming
(or better still devise their own library/reference/cataloging-
oriented compiler language) and librarians who will assist publishers in creating the tools they need in a way which will permit more
effective and efficient reference service.
    In my opinion, we should not stand by while linguists, mathe-
maticians, and systems engineers redesign our own library-
information systems. We should be involved in plans for the reference tools, which eventually will all be machine-generated for
purely economic reasons.

----
[11] Don R. Swanson, *op. cit.,* p.10, 11.

Certain areas of research and development suggest themselves if we consider contributing to the development of machine-generated reference tools and improved reference services. These projects should be carried out by research teams which include librarians. The teams could:

1. Survey the most typical reference-work activities and the linkage of this work with various reference tools. Rothstein's comments[12] on core titles of encyclopedias, dictionaries, and almanacs in published literature reference work are worth noting here. The survey could be done by type of library, as well as by type of work, on a local and regional basis (similar to a suggestion by Verner Clapp).
2. Survey the major reference-tool publishers; determine the feasibility of increasing the data bank of machine-readable "reference" information; and estimate the changeover costs necessary to provide by-products of the type described. Such a study should include a cost-savings survey in libraries which would use these tools instead of conventional tools.
3. Plan and implement a demonstration project involving several libraries, in which machine-readable catalogs would be integrated with some machine-readable reference tools. The libraries would have a reference staff and user population capable of being trained to work with such an automated system. Perform experiments and monitor use to determine new approaches to information, new types of reference/information activity, and so forth.
4. Experiment with programmed teaching machines at appropriate points in public libraries, college campuses, and research laboratories to study ways of improving access to available information or referral services.

No doubt many enterprising librarians in the audience have thought of many more projects which could make their work easier and the use of the library by their patrons more rewarding. Machine-generated reference tools are not a panacea; but the potential for new approaches to reference/information work, as well as greater ease in human communication, seem limitless with them and almost impossible without them.

---

[12] Samuel Rothstein, "The Measurement and Evaluation of Reference Service," *Library Trends*, 12:463 (Jan., 1964).

SUMMARY

1. We need to stress a coordinated approach to information system and network development—from *origin* of information (author's manuscript to editor/publisher) to *use* of information (in library, research worker's office, and the like).
2. We need to combine efforts and avoid *redo* of input operations (automatic typesetting for publisher; machine-readable cataloging for library; data compilations in information centers).
3. We should follow the *principle of least action* in information system.
4. We should follow the *principle of by-product data generation* in machine-generated data.
5. We must make *provision for combinability and flexibility* of information records.

Comment

Edwin B. Colburn

We have heard about the problem of the vast explosion of materials coming to us and the bibliographic control of them. I am sure that we are all aware that, in the past five years or so, publishing output in this country, in terms of number of titles, has doubled. We have now reached about the same level as that of Great Britain, and those of you who have recently received your 1963/64 *CBI* cumulation know that we have had to divide it into two volumes because it was just not feasible to put it in one volume. We have had some complaints, but we have explained that had we not put it in two volumes, the binding problem would have been manifestly increased. The binding would have had to be done by hand, making it much more costly and much slower. Also, if we had put in one volume all the material that went into that *CBI*, you would be using it at risk of life and limb.

The same thing is true of periodicals. It has been stated this afternoon that some 70,000-75,000 periodicals are being issued. In the case of both books and periodicals, I am not always sure that all are worthwhile. The other day in the office I noticed a book, a sizable volume, at least two inches thick. The title was *Mosquitoes of the Southwest Pacific*. I suppose some day someone might want it, but it seemed to me that it offered more information about mosquitoes than I would like to have. The H. W. Wilson Company is currently indexing some 1500 periodicals. If we were to take the

Edwin B. Colburn, Vice-President and Chief of Indexing Services of the H. W. Wilson Company, has had experience in both public and university libraries. He has held many offices in ALA Divisions and in the Council of National Library Associations and has been a member of the Decimal Classification Editorial Policy Committee.

other indexing services and add them all together, we would still
be covering only a relatively small proportion of what is being
produced. I also fear that we are covering a small proportion of
what really should be indexed, but there are limitations.

I am assuming the present situation, not defending it. We have
had certain problems raised this afternoon, and we have also had
some potential solutions offered. How valid those solutions may be
I am not sure, because I am not sufficiently familiar with the potentialities. But, if we assume the present situation, we have, first of
all, the limitation of cost. There have been times during the past
two days that I have wondered, trembling just a little bit, if the H.
W. Wilson Company were going to publish indexes in the years
ahead. Then I stopped to think about the fact that, back at the office,
we have addressograph plates for more than 70,000 libraries which
are buying something or other from the company. Now, obviously,
you know as well as I do that, if there are 70,000 libraries buying
Wilson indexes, catalog cards, or standard catalogs, many of them
are very small libraries. And they are still going to need indexes.
The library in Errol, New Hampshire, or in Caribou, Maine, is not
going to be close enough to any other center or source of information to take care of the day-to-day needs of either adults or students. These libraries are still going to want the *Readers' Guide*
or the *Abridged Readers' Guide* or some of the other indexes that
they are now getting; so I am reassured. But I also realize that
the fact that there are so many of these small libraries means we
must think about costs. Their budgets are still limited, despite
the burgeoning of library budgets generally. The librarians might
very well find themselves unable to purchase the basic tools they
need if indexing services were to expand too greatly and increase
their costs too much.

Now, to publications sold on a service basis. The service basis
has been criticized from time to time, but it has also been defended.
I think the best defense for it can be easily illustrated. A number
of years ago, when we studied the *Industrial Arts Index*, we found
that the average cost to the subscribers was $50. Seventy-five per-
cent of the libraries were getting it at less than the average cost
and, of those, probably one third or more were paying the absolute
minimum price, which at that time was $15. Now picture what
would happen if we were to put the index on a flat rate of $50. Most
of the libraries paying $15 would say, "We cannot afford to pay
more than three times as much," and they would drop out and the
average cost would go up. Then others would say, "Well, we are
paying $25, but we cannot pay $60," and the average cost would go
up again when they dropped out. Eventually, there would be no subscribers to the index; so we feel we must maintain a service basis

on certain publications. What does this mean? It means that the individual library or libraries that receive a certain periodical have to help share the cost of indexing that periodical.

When the Committee on Wilson Indexes of this Reference Services Division made a study of the *Art Index,* they found several magazines which they thought were excellent and should be indexed. They made a list of these and asked if we could give them an idea of how much it would cost to index them and then see how much the subscription rate would have to be. We found one periodical that was so seldom held and would require so much indexing that it would cost each library that received it $400. Starting from there and building the charges of the other magazines on top of that creates a pretty steep bill—something that would be impossible for libraries to afford. This is something we must take into account as we consider what we can do.

Then there are people who sometimes say: "Why can't you have a larger index?" Let's take the *Applied Science and Technology Index* as an example. When this was started in 1958, we carefully estimated the number of entries that would be required in a year to index the magazines covered in the index. We estimated that we would probably have about 75,000 entries. When we took a recount about a year ago, we found we had underestimated by 10,000. There are two factors that enter into this. One of them is the increase in money around the country which can be used in advertising. The other is the desire of the publishers to balance the editorial material and the advertising; so there are more articles, and more indexing is required. We have reached the point where we barely get this index out each month. If you are familiar with government regulations for the Post Office Department, you know that indexes which are mailed second class (and we like to send them second class because this saves you money) must be mailed in the month in which they are dated. Some months, we are just worried to death for fear of not getting the *Applied Science and Technology Index* in the mail by March 31, or April 30, or whatever it may be.

People say: "Well, just hire more indexers!" The solution is not as easy as that. Reference has been made this afternoon to the fact that there is a human variation among indexers. They do not all approach an article the same way or give the same subjects. So there must be one person who has final responsibility for this and also for the establishment of new subject headings, a great deal of which has to be done in indexing periodicals. One person can do only so much. You cannot expect former conditions. Miss Potter, the first employee of the company and editor of several publications in successive years, used to work as many hours at home as she did

at the office, and she was never paid for it. People just don't want
to do that any more, and we don't want them to.

There is also the question of how much of a printing load a company can carry. With the number of periodical indexes and catalogs
we have, we must constantly be working to arrange our schedules to
get the publications out. Unfortunately, in recent years, we have had
to have some of our printing done outside. This, again, increases
costs because we are paying the outside printer's overhead and profit.

Then there is a question of demand. As you know, the Wilson
indexes are governed on a very democratic basis, so that subscribers
can decide what is to be indexed. Some persons will come forward
and say; "You should index this," or "You should index that." But
when you put "this" or "that" up to subscribers, they don't want it,
they turn it down, they say it is not worth indexing. Perhaps there
is not as much of a need here as we may have pictured.

Reference has been made to timeliness. This is a problem of
which we are very much aware, a problem which we have been trying to lick. I do not want to make excuses; please, do not think I am
on the defensive. I would like to point out just one thing. Those of
you who subscribe to three or four or half a dozen periodicals know
that occasionally the subscription records get mixed up, and sud-
denly your copy does not come. But when you are subscribing to
1500 periodicals, this happens frequently. When the records are
finally straightened out, you get six issues all at once and you index
them. We have found that, if one August issue of a periodical is
listed in the January number of the index, although the rest are all
December issues, people see that one August issue and say that we
are far behind in indexing.

Miss Harris made reference to the question of author entries,
particularly in the *Business Periodicals Index* and the *Applied Science and Technology Index*. The subject has arisen before, and the
question has always been whether the subscribers want author entries or would rather have more periodicals covered. In every
case, they have said they wanted more periodicals covered. So we
are a little bit caught there.

People sometimes ask about selective indexing. I feel two
ways and two things about this. One, you have to read the article
anyway before you decide whether or not you are going to index it,
whether it is worth indexing. By the time you have read it, you
might as well give it a subject heading and go on. Let me illustrate
the other point this way. When I was at the New York Public Library, one of my jobs was to sort gifts. These gifts would come in,
and some of them were awful. Some were extremely specialized,
and I would look at them and think that we didn't need them. Then
I would say, "Some day somebody may want that," so we would keep

it. An indexer tends more and more to think the same way, and by and by he is not doing selective indexing but is indexing everything there is.

I am concerned about a problem that has been referred to this afternoon—the duplication of indexing. The Committee on Wilson Indexes is currently studying the *Business Periodicals Index* and the *Applied Science and Technology Index*. They send out questionnaires; the replies come in at the office; and we tabulate the statistical information, including the suggestions of titles to be considered for indexing. I was interested, as I looked at the titles suggested for the *Applied Science and Technology Index*, to find any number of titles indexed in eight or nine or ten places. One is indexed in twelve different places at the present time. I, personally, although I have no voice in the matter (the committee and the subscribers will face this problem)—I, personally, question whether we should add a thirteenth. The committee has endeavored, throughout a series of studies of our indexes, to try to avoid duplication wherever possible. And the committee has succeeded to a remarkable extent in getting away from duplication by constantly calling to the attention of the subscribers, and urging them to vote for, items that are not indexed elsewhere, that are worthy of indexing, that have permanent reference value, and so forth. A great deal of duplication has been eliminated. However, there are always people who say: "I want to have it in the index I take, and I don't want to have to take another index. I can't afford it. My budget won't allow it." So we are under that pressure, too.

Now the question of how we can possibly use the methods about which Mrs. Atherton was talking this afternoon has given me and my colleagues a great deal of pause. We have wondered much about it; we do not have closed minds. We feel, as I indicated earlier, that we have to continue to produce printed indexes for the small libraries that do not have the machines needed for other types of indexes. They do not have access to centralized places or sources that they can go to readily and quickly. We did try an experiment in cooperation with Library U.S.A. Our experience was, I think, somewhat less than satisfactory. We were approached, prior to the Seattle conference, and asked if we would provide indexing copy from *Readers' Guide* to be put into a computer so that people could go to the exhibit and ask for a list of periodicals on a subject. The whole plan fell through because the necessary computer was not forthcoming.

The idea was revived for the library at the New York World's Fair. Joe Becker came up and talked to us, and we said we would be glad to cooperate in any way we could. At first, the directors said they would take the periodicals indexed in the *Readers' Guide*.

When they saw the volume involved, however, they said they could not accommodate all that in the computer but would take the periodicals in the *Abridged Readers' Guide*. They took copies of that along to study, but, later, they came back saying they could not accommodate all that and so would pick out eighteen magazines and take those only. We started preparing copy for them in October of 1963. The first problem they encountered was that the computer takes only seventy-five subjects; we have a potential of some 40,000 subject headings which can be used in the *Readers' Guide*. That sort of reassured us that we knew more than the machine. We said: "All right, but we can't break the headings down the way you need them, because we don't know what your subject headings are going to be." So they had to redo all this, and then they ran into some difficulties in programming. We had started preparing the copy for them in October, 1963, and they finally got it into the computer in July, 1965, shortly before the Fair ended. Now I do not mean to imply that the computer is an impractical thing, but it was impractical in that particular case.

We have recently made use of different means of printing with the *Union List of Serials*. When the Joint Committee on the *Union List of Serials* approached us about publishing the list, we indicated that we were willing to do so. They said: "One qualification we are going to make is that the printing must be done in England." It seems that Balding and Mansell in England have some kind of camera which, to my knowledge, no one here has seen. They are keeping it a very close secret. They used it to produce the *British Museum Catalog*, and they used it to produce the *Union List of Serials*. Those of you who have bought the *Union List of Serials* at a price of $125 can thank Balding and Mansell for some of that, because approximately $100,000 was saved in the printing of that work by the use of this method.

As yet, we have not found anything that will solve all of our problems. At first, I thought this was probably just ignorance on our part. However, when we were making plans for the experiment with Library U.S.A., we talked at some length with Mortimer Taube, who indicated a definite interest in trying to solve our problems by some mechanical means. He took our indexes back to Washington to study them very carefully and, after several weeks, returned them to us and said: "We are not ready for you yet." This does not mean that we are not thinking about the future. One of these days, you may get Wilson indexes and other indexes prepared in the way Mrs. Atherton has suggested.

Discussion

Adams: I would like to assure Mrs. Atherton that there is at least one other publisher in the room. I am speaking on behalf of a rather extensive publisher of indexes, The National Library of Medicine, which does depend on the computer for production, and which has found it practicable for even larger file sizes than those of the H. W. Wilson Company. And, incidentally, speaking as publisher to publisher, your remarks about some of the problems involved in indexing literature really struck a familiar note. We have identical problems: the problem of journal selection, the problem of file size, and the problems of skilled personnel; all of these we are experiencing.

I am wholly in sympathy with the point Mrs. Atherton was making. By courtesy of the H. W. Wilson Company, I would like to quote myself from the April issue of the *Wilson Library Bulletin:* "The underlying concept [of MEDLARS] is that a large data base, or pool of machine-readable bibliographic unit records, can be drawn upon to provide multiple bibliographic current-awareness services of the type required by modern science."[1]

Back in 1961, when Dr. F. B. Rogers originally planned MEDLARS, he did specify, as a secondary objective of the system, the production of multiple recurring bibliographies, or specialized indexes, to be drawn from a centralized pool of data. We are now producing some seven of these and have approximately twenty more under development. I might cite a few of those that are actually now in production, some of which

[1] Scott Adams, "Bibliographic Organization in the Biomedical Sciences," *Wilson Library Bulletin,* 40:718 (Apr., 1966).

we publish and some of which are published by other organizations through arrangement with us. We publish, for example, the *Bibliography of Medical Reviews*. We prepare the *Index to Dental Literature*, but it is published by the American Dental Association. The *Cerebrovascular Bibliography* is published by our sister agency, the National Institute of Neurological Diseases and Blindness; the *Index of Rheumatology*, by the American Rheumatism Association; the *Bibliography of Medical Education*, by the Association of American Medical Colleges in their journal; and, finally, as of tomorrow, the first issue of the *International Nursing Index* will be off the press, published by the American Nursing Association. Now behind all of this is the concept of dipping into a very large data bank or pool of tape-stored unit bibliographic citations, which now totals approximately 450,000. Concurrent with *Index Medicus* publication, we repackage its citations for the purpose of producing specialized bibliographies within particular or broad fields of professional activities or of research related to medicine.

I will stop at this point and say that this is not easily done, because it must be done using precise terms of the subject-heading authority list or thesaurus which, if you are using a vocabulary system, as we are, controls the entire system. Defining the complex requirements of any area of science in terms of this control vocabulary is a considerable intellectual exercise. It took one bright young investigator, working with a team of three scientific advisers, a year and a half simply to specify the combination of subject headings that made up the total interest of one field. But, nonetheless, we are undertaking these projects; we have some twenty more of them under development. We are also providing recurring-demand search services, identifying certain topics which individuals wish searched, let us say, once a month, and regular current-awareness service in the form of a bibliography. Similarly, we are publishing selected literature searches. We select about half a dozen searches a week which seem worthy of publication; rerun them through Grace, the photocomposing device; publish them in a small edition; and advertise their availability in the principal journals.

The point I want to make is that we are actually experiencing what Mrs. Atherton has described—the creation of a large centralized data pool of mechanized bibliographic citations and the utilization of this pool for a whole variety of purposes. We plan to share this capability with others. Under our program of decentralization of **MEDLARS**, we intend to

make tapes available to universities so that they will be able
to provide at local levels the same kind of recurring bibliographies which we are attempting to provide at the national
level. We are working with national associations and with societies which have national distribution. The universities will
be working with their own departments and with affiliated institutes to provide a more localized distribution. I do not think
we have begun to realize the dimensions of exploitation and the
potential social utility that this national resource has. We
have started in a modest way; we are doing our best to live
this philosophy, but I think there is a great deal more to be
done.

Dubester: May I address a question to Scott Adams? When the
MEDLARS system was planned, you all did an exemplary job
of developing a planning stage and a designing stage which
specified the system requirements, selected the computer
configuration, designated the output, and so on. At that time,
you had not planned for the type of decentralized system into
which you are now moving.

Adams: That was specified as one of the secondary objectives,
Henry.

Dubester: My question is this: If you had to do the whole thing
over again today, had to set up your requirements in the light
of what you now know, and were free to do things differently,
what would you do in the light of your experience? Would you
do anything differently? Would you change your requirements?
This last question concerns the standardization problem that
ensued after you had made your fix on certain types of hardware.

Adams: The answer is yes; we certainly would change today, and
I might take a moment to explain why. Frankly, MEDLARS is
antiquated. This area of technology has developed so fast that,
in computer technology, it is almost as if we were back in the
Dark Ages. When MEDLARS was frozen in 1961, we made a
very thorough investigation of the capabilities of all system
hardware configurations then available. We knew the volume
we had to process. At that point in time, the Minneapolis
Honeywell answered our volume specifications best. Unfortunately, the Minneapolis 800 is limited to a computer language
that is uncommon. Therefore, when we wanted to decentralize,
we had to reprogram the system into a more common language
so that the types of computers generally used on university
campuses could search the tapes. We have done this; and programs will be available to universities so that the tapes can be
very widely used. This is a long, roundabout answer to the

question. Today, the computer market has so developed its storage capabilities that we would have a much wider choice, and we would certainly use that freedom of choice. We would go to a system where we did not have to reprogram, where we could do all our programming in a language commonly used and, hence, available to more people.

Murray: I would like to address a question to Mrs. Atherton. As a by-product to the making of bibliographies or indexes in paper form, there would have to be machine-readable material, which I assume would be tapes. For an institution which subscribes to the paper copy and which would also like to get the tapes (to enable searching through a machine instead of through an indefinite number of alphabets), the problem of cost has arisen. I wonder if anyone would comment on the cost of such tapes to a subscriber who was already buying the indexes in paper form. Has any thought been given to this?

Atherton: The costs are possibly the same. They may be hidden, but they are still there.

Murray: I meant the cost to the consumer, not the producer. Government agencies are often very good to us in covering costs. But one index, we found, was out of reach; it was done on the basis of the number of people who would use the index. Although we could afford the paper, we could not afford the tape.

Adams: I think I can give you an honest answer to that. The cost of the tapes themselves, of course, is minimal. A reel of tape costs about $50. To copy, at least in our system, the six reels of tape per year is going to cost about $1000, plus or minus. So a year's supply of indexing, i.e., 175,000-200,000 citations, at just the incremental cost of manufacture of duplicating tapes, would cost around $1000. However, with all respect to a large enterprise that is marketing tapes, this price does not reflect the sizable, and I mean sizable, cost of inputting the information, the actual indexing itself. This is where governmental units may have a slight advantage. Government regulations require them to charge incremental costs. *Chemical Abstracts,* or any other group distributing tapes privately, must recover some of the costs and the overhead of initial indexing activity.

Murray: These would have been recovered in the paper copy, would they not?

Atherton: The cost would have to be spread over the original input because it would be used for different purposes. It could be spread over the subscription price to each of the by-products. Then the cost would not have to be borne only by the printed copy or only by the people receiving the machine-readable copy.

I would like to comment on this cost of input, especially within the context of science and technology. This does not apply to some of the other fields. At the American Institute of Physics, the present input costs of publishing the journal are not borne by the subscriber, because of the page-charge philosophy which governs all the publication efforts in science and technology. The government says that every person who gets a research project grant from the United States Government should put one percent of his research budget aside to fund the cost of publishing the research results. So the cost of the actual typesetting of the paper is borne by something called the page charge, not by the subscriber to the journal. And this, I am sure, will be part of the philosophy underlying the machine-readable copy as well as the present printed copy. A subscriber will then be able to get, for example, 10,000 pages of the *Physical Review* per year for something like $40 because the cost of putting it into type will already be covered by the cost of the research that is being reported.

Adams: I would not want anyone to go away from here thinking that for $1000 a year it is possible to get into searching operations. Supporting the manpower, machine rental charges, and so forth needed to conduct any type of extensive search operation —in one of our decentralized centers, for example—would cost a minimum of $75,000 a year.

Frame: My question has to do with subject headings. We are presently keyed primarily to Library of Congress subject headings, and we find that in our data-processing and computer contemplations we have a great deal of difficulty figuring out what kind of subject headings are going to be usable and are keywords which can be put into any further kinds of compilations. Is there any organization which is currently working on a new list of library-type subject headings which lend themselves to computer-type productions?

Atherton: I do not know how to begin, because I am rather excited about what is going on. There is nothing magical about so-called computer thesauri as compared to typical library subject-heading lists. This is what you see in the field if you watch. People who started out with "uniterm" and then "coordinate indexing" are now almost back to what we would call "alphabetic classified subject headings." When I do my work, as I have just done, on computerizing or creating machine-readable records of the subject headings in *Physics Abstracts*, as far as I am concerned it is no different from the *Sears List of Subject Headings*. In fact, when we print it out, it looks very much like that list. There is nothing magical about having

to convert your language, as you are presently using it in the
library, into a form that is more easily handled by the machine.
I am sure this was the reason for wanting to reduce the 40,000
subject headings of the H. W. Wilson Company down to 75. But
this is not necessarily a requirement of the machine that has
to be imposed upon your system. We do not have time to go
into detail, but the picture of taking something like the Library
of Congress subject headings, putting them into machine-
readable form, and using them in a mechanized retrieval system is not as black as you might think. Luckily, I can report
that the Library of Congress as well as other large academic
libraries are already in the process of grappling with this
problem.

Busha: I have a question in reference to what Mr. Mohrhardt said
this morning about the Library of Congress; it also has application to what Mrs. Atherton said this afternoon. How can we
develop a national reference network plan without reorganizing
the present system of federal libraries and by law making the
Library of Congress a truly national library which could not
only be responsible for the nationwide supervision of library
services and programs, but also serve as the national voice of
libraries and as an organ for nationwide library research? In
my estimation, we need a national library which would be a
library for librarians, responsible for supervision of the national reference resource system. I think such a library is
necessary because of all the observations made here in this
conference about machine-generated reference tools, information systems, and automation and various innovations in automation.

In reference to Mr. Mohrhardt's statement about the
Library of Congress not being able to serve as a national
library because of its commitment to Congress, I would like
to point out that many state libraries operate on a miniature
Library of Congress basis in their states. They provide reference service to the legislative and executive branches of the
state government, while at the same time acting as state libraries. It is my opinion that we need federal legislation to create a
national library organ which would incorporate and greatly extend
the present Library of Congress. Is this feasible? Is it realistic?
If it is realistic, what can librarians do to bring it about?

Adams: I think that both Mr. Mohrhardt and Mr. Lorenz have already left the meeting. I would like to remind you of what Mr.
Lorenz said to you this morning—that you are both constituents
and librarians. If you believe that some form of legislative
action is required, it is up to you to make that known. Another

point relates to Mr. Mohrhardt's suggestion that at present
COSATI is very much interested in feedback from the library
community to some of its proposals. You will recall that the
COSATI report does deal with a strong and effective national
library system.

Dubester: The situation, as I see it, is something on this order.
Being the library to Congress is not the factor which keeps
the Library of Congress from being a national library. The
real limiting factor is that this relationship has put the budget
for the Library of Congress into legislative appropriation. I
think that Congress wants to keep its own budget down; when
people talk about the amount that Congress is appropriating
for itself, they are including the budget for the Library of
Congress. Various proposals have been advanced to change
this. In 1946, Metcalf was chairman of a committee that recommended legislation which Congress turned down. Luther
Evans was chairman of a Brookings study which recommended
a shift of the Library of Congress to the executive branch.
This idea was not accepted. But interestingly enough, what is
happening is that Congress is developing its own support
mechanisms to give the Library of Congress the armament to
accomplish its national library function. It is appropriating
funds for the Office of Education, so that that Office can assume a broad international acquisitions function. It is doing
this; and it has done the same in minor areas. Congress is,
practically speaking, recognizing the need for a national library
and is supporting the Library of Congress increasingly in that
direction.

Aspnes: I want to ask a question to which I am sure there is no
answer; yet I think it should be asked. It concerns economics.
Miss Harris listed some of the many tools that the reference
librarian uses and mentioned some of the needs that are not
being filled. Mrs. Atherton described some of the work being
done at the American Institute of Physics and in other areas.
All of us know that indexes are the keys to our kingdom; in
that respect, the market for indexes is a seller's market, but
it is a limited one. Now, the question is: Could the National
Library of Medicine's MEDLARS project have been carried
out by the Wilson Company, with the restriction under which it
has to work—that of making a profit; by *Chemical Abstracts;*
or by the American Institute of Physics, a nonprofit institution
which still has to equalize the costs? I doubt that it could
have been. Therefore, is it not obvious that, in the future, the
federal government is going to have to be the only source for
good reference tools that are beyond the economic ability of
any private or nonprofit organization?

Adams: I would like to risk a reply. I take exception to that word
"only" that you used. I think that the federal government is
vitally concerned, particularly in science and technology, with
bibliographic access to literature. A certain amount of this is
accomplished "in house" by organizations such as ours or
Foster Mohrhardt's National Agricultural Library. But there
are a number of support programs, including that of the National Science Foundation, directed toward the improvement of
bibliographic services in areas of statutory responsibility.
The problem arises, you see, in attempting to match the total
national needs, as does the H. W. Wilson Company, for example,
with the areas of responsibility of the several agencies. It is a
somewhat imperfect match because the missions and purposes
of the agencies are limited by law, and they cannot provide general support across the board. For example, in these days of
scientific revolution, there is far more support for bibliographic service in science and technology than there can be
for the humanities, much as I, personally, regret this.

Dalton: I do not have a question, Mr. Chairman, but I do have a
comment on Mr. Aspnes' question. The Reference Services
Division has a committee on bibliography which has been assigned the problem of finding funds for bibliographical publication of all kinds. The problem which we encountered when
we were given this assignment was that funds were not forthcoming from publishers and that foundations were not willing
to give funds, either. We are even now working on the problem
of how we relate the activities of the national libraries, the
funds of the national government and the foundations, and the
needs of the makers and users of bibliographies. When we
visited the foundations to talk about this problem, the people
there said substantially what they said several years ago when
the foundations went out of the library business—that the bibliographical demands on them had been such that if they liqui-
dated, turned over all their money to the needs of bibliography,
and went out of business, they were sure that the libraries
would be back where they were before within ten years. They
insisted that the problem was too big for them, that only the
national government could handle it. While we have no solution,
we are quite sure, Mr. Aspnes, that this *is* a federal problem,
and we are even now trying to find some mechanism for getting
started with a problem that we know must be solved at that
level.

Information Storage and Retrieval Systems

Development of Storage and Retrieval Systems
                              Joseph Becker   151

Using Accumulated Knowledge
                    Emmanuel G. Mesthene   157

Comment   *Grieg Aspnes*   165

Discussion   168

Development of Storage and Retrieval Systems

Joseph Becker

In my class on library automation at Catholic University, I can always rely on one bright student to ask, "How are computers used in reference work?" For someone like myself, firmly committed to library automation and overflowing with friendly feelings toward machines, it is embarrassing to respond to this question by back-pedaling; but that is exactly what I must do. Library reference work demands a high order of intellectual activity, and its subtleties have thus far proved too elusive for computer programming. I say "thus far," because I believe the time will come when some ingenious person will supply the missing algorithm that will make machines as vital to the support of the reference function as they already are to technical processing. There are many obstacles to computer progress in the reference area, but they can be removed through continuing research and development. What are the bottle-necks? What have been the results of experimental work to date? What are the prospects for the future?

The first bottleneck results from a technical limitation that prevents the rapid conversion of printed matter into machine-readable form. In other words, the computer can be of little help to the reference librarian until the data with which it must work have been put into digital form. The second concerns the lack of new intellectual concepts of information organization that are significantly better than the traditional methods of alphabetic subject

Joseph Becker, since July, 1966, has been with EDUCOM on a full-time basis. After a period with the New York Public Library, he held various positions with the U.S. government, most recently as a Director of Computer Operations. Mr. Becker has written many articles on automation and computer technology and is the coauthor, with R. M. Hayes, of the text, *Information Storage and Retrieval* (Wiley, 1963).

151

headings and decimal classification. The real problem is to develop computer programs that not only *organize* information by subject but also are capable of logically *reorganizing* stored information in order to respond to the changing needs of library users. When this has been done, it may become possible to extract underlying patterns of meaning from a complex mass of information. This is the ultimate objective.

The term "machine-readable" denotes the representation of nonnumerical information as codes on punched cards, on punched paper tape, or on magnetic tape. In numerical data processing, the volume of data entering a computer is generally small, and very often the computer expresses its solution as a single number. However, when we process the full text of journal articles, books, or even catalog cards by computer, the volume of data that must first be transposed to machine-readable form is enormous.

The routine way to convert nonnumerical information into machine-readable code is to re-key the printed information one letter at a time, using a key-punch machine or a tape-operated typewriter. Both methods are slow, prohibitively expensive, and prone to error. To overcome these difficulties, character-recognition machines that scan the printed page and automatically convert each letter, word, and sentence to machine-readable code are being developed. This is not a far-fetched idea. Character-recognition machines already exist that can scan a printed page and convert the ten numerals, special symbols, and the upper- and lower-case letters of a prescribed type font into equivalent machine code. For example, the squiggles we see in the lower left-hand corner of our personal bank checks are machine-readable, as are the embossed numerals on our gasoline credit cards.

Published material is printed in a variety of type fonts, styles, and alphabets. As librarians, we are well aware of how impractical it would be to attempt to compel publishers to use a standard type font. Therefore, the technical challenge is to develop a machine capable of reading intermixed fonts, and this is an overwhelming assignment. Until this objective is achieved, however, it is unlikely that large quantities of printed information will be machine-readable. It logically follows that machines are not apt to be of much help to the reference librarian until a much larger corpus of data can find its way into the computer.

On the assumption that much of tomorrow's information will be produced in machine-readable form, experimental work in textual analysis through computer programming has been under way for many years. These experiments are of interest to the reference librarian, because they illustrate how computers can be used to perform certain intellectual tasks. For example, in the early

1950's, UNIVAC compiled a complete Bible concordance by computer. This compilation was a straightforward alphabetical sorting task for the computer, once the original text was machine-readable. Today, the preparation of a *computer concordance* from any machine-readable text is a simple and speedy process. In 1958, Hans Peter Luhn wrote a computer program for indexing documents automatically. Mr. Luhn's source of machine-readable text was *Time* magazine. The same machine-readable, punched paper tape which *Time* used to drive an automatic linotype machine was adapted by Luhn as input to his computer-programming experiments. His basic program worked as follows:

1. Each word in the text was assigned a consecutive number by the computer. The purpose of this "housekeeping" was to provide Luhn with a method for reconstructing the text in its original sequence in the unhappy event that the computer accidentally scrambled the words.
2. Luhn then set up an alphabetical table containing the common prepositions, articles, pronouns, and conjunctions and embedded these words in his program. (Louis Ridenour once referred to these words as the "connective tissue" of language.) As each text word entered the computer, it was compared to the list of common words. Exact matches were shunted to one part of computer memory, while the residual words—i.e., the nouns, verbs, adjectives, and adverbs (which Luhn called "notion" words)—were collected in another part of memory.
3. Next, the computer program alphabetized the notion words and kept count of the number of times each was used by the author.
4. Finally, the program ranked the words in order by frequency of use and printed out the highest six. Luhn considered these to be his index terms.

   You may feel, as I do, that this statistical analysis of an author's use of words represents an unprofessional approach to indexing. However, since Luhn's *automatic-indexing* experiment, other researchers have added a second table to the program to incorporate the standard headings and "see also" references of a particular subject list. This expanded program causes the machine to compare the most frequently used words in the text with the standard list of subject headings and to print out only those terms which match and are thus known to be valid in the system. In this case, the judgment made by the computer is a logical one rather than an evaluative decision. Rejected terms are printed separately, to be reviewed later by a librarian as part of normal subject-heading maintenance procedure.

Another computer program traces the words used most frequently by an author back to the sentences in which they first appeared. This program causes the computer to print out the complete text of the five sentences containing the greatest number of high-ranking words. The resultant paragraph has been referred to as an *automatic abstract*. Here, again, opinions differ about the professional value of this program. In technical fields, where vocabularies are precise, the automatic abstract seems more helpful than in the social sciences, where meaning is often obscured by nebulous language.

Automatic dissemination or searching is a fourth technique. In this program, the words of the text are compared singly or in combination with a list of terms specified by one or more users. Thus, as the content of new articles enters the computer, the program logically determines, on a selective basis, which incoming articles are of particular interest to users served by the library. These "interest profiles" are modified from time to time to reflect shifts in user need or emphasis. The same method can be employed for making retrospective reference searches of the mass of data as the need arises.

It should be noted that research work in the area I have described has not been confined to English texts; similar work has been done in other languages. If, for example, it were possible to translate foreign languages by machine, then the same programs which apply to the indexing, abstracting, disseminating, and searching of English would be applicable without change.

Machine translation has passed through three phases. Ten years ago, computer programs were written that performed word-for-word translation. These automatic dictionaries produced stumbling literal translations because the computer supplied, with unfailing generosity, every possible English equivalent for each word in the foreign text. Later on, linguists analyzed the syntax of the foreign language, developing reliable rules for correct word order, proper stem endings, prepositional phrases, and so forth. Most recent work has concerned semantic analysis. Because meaning is generally hidden in contextual interpretation, the absence of rules defies programming by machine. While today's machine translation is superior to the literal translation of a decade ago, it is still a long way from smooth prose.

A current trend within the library profession is to produce catalog data that are machine-readable. Verner Clapp, in his opening address, spoke of an on-line national reference system, and this implies an electronic store of bibliographic information

at the national level. Foster Mohrhardt expanded this idea by describing the types of network arrangements that may be suitable
for libraries of the future. Production of machine-readable catalog data is practical because it can be captured as a by-product of
typing in the catalog department. Granted that we must first agree
on standardized format and content, the gradual stockpiling of such
data would eventually lead to the creation of a union catalog which
could serve reference stations in many libraries through a network. A microcosm of this idea exists today in the MEDLARS
system at the National Library of Medicine. The library now sup-
plies duplicate magnetic tapes and is planning to offer remote-
inquiry service in the future.

No discussion of the technologies pertinent to the field of information storage and retrieval would be complete without consideration of the role of communications. In the early 1950's, RCA
conducted a demonstration of Ultrafax at the Library of Congress.
A film copy of *Gone with the Wind* was sent over communication
lines to a receiving point in a distant city. This facsimile transmission heralded the use of communication facilities for the
transfer of visual data from one point to another. Video recording
and transmission provide still another medium for sending graphic
information over great distances.

Retrieval of digital and graphic information at a distance pre-
supposes the availability of an interconnected communications network. On this assumption, research has been conducted to explore
the relationship between man and machine in order to define more
clearly the division of tasks between them. This, in turn, has led
to further research in the area of on-line systems, which establishes direct communication between the man at an input-output
console and the computer. The Massachusetts Institute of Technology has led the research effort to place at a user's fingertips
the communications equipment needed to interrogate a large store
of information under the control of a computer while numerous
other users are simultaneously using it.

Dr. M. M. Kessler of the M.I.T. Library has developed a
working model of an on-line retrieval system that can handle as
many as one hundred remote consoles over ordinary telephone
wire. Elements of data from the literature of a selected group of
physics journals constitute the data base. The interaction between
the user and the system is free of intermediaries and is accomplished by means of a language very close to natural English.

Demonstrations of remote retrieval by computer were also
featured at the Library U.S.A. exhibit produced by the American
Library Association for the U.S. Pavilion at the New York World's
Fair of 1964-65. Any person with access to a teletype machine

was able to interrogate ALA's electronic computer at the New
York World's Fair for selected essays, bibliographies, translations, and current periodical references by subject.

From the above review of development activities, three clear
objectives emerge: (1) to find automatic means of converting
printed data to machine-readable language; (2) to enhance intellectual access to information; and (3) to communicate and display information rapidly in a form suitable for local use. The continuing
evolution of unconventional subject-classification systems, the application of computers, and the use of advanced communications
techniques represent the principal means of achieving the goal.

Lest I have generated a sense of inadequacy in the audience
with all this machine talk, I wish to close this morning with a quotation from a recent essay by Professor W. T. Williams of the
faculty of the University of Southampton. Professor Williams
finds that man enjoys three advantages over the computer that he
may well retain even into the distant future: he weighs less than
the computer; he requires far less energy than does the computer;
and he "is the only computer yet designed which can be produced
entirely by unskilled labour."[1]

[1] W. T. Williams, "Computers as Botanists," in Barbara R. F. Kyle, ed.,
Focus on Information and Communication; papers by Rupert Crawshay-
Williams ₁and others₁ (London: Aslib, 1965), p.86.

Using Accumulated Knowledge

Emmanuel G. Mesthene

In defense against the fate that often attends a speaker who is
scheduled at the end of a long program of speeches, I should like
to try to shock you into attention by suggesting the imminent de-
mise of the profession of the librarian as we have known it. This
might appear the sheerest ingratitude toward both my hosts and
audience here today, but I am hoping and gambling that I can have
them and you with me, rather than against me, by the time I have
finished.

I had a conversation recently with my friend and colleague,
Douglas Bryant, at Harvard. The subject was our concern to organize a useful information function for the Harvard Program on Technology and Society, which I head. We had agreed, over the months,
that this should not be a traditional library or research collection,
but rather a working "man-book" system that could serve as an active communication link between the people working under the program and the relevant documentation and allied research work,
wherever they might be and wherever work was going on.

"But that is not a job that a librarian can handle," I said to
Doug, and he replied, "You're wrong, Manny! What you mean is
that it is a job that requires a *good* librarian." And thereby hangs
my tale. Both of us, clearly, were seeing the same thing, though
we had arrived at it by different routes and called it by different

Emmanuel G. Mesthene is Executive Director of the Program on Technology and Society, Harvard University. After teaching assignments at Adelphi
College and Columbia University, Dr. Mesthene was on the staff of the Economics Department of the Rand Corporation and then for short terms held
assignments as Consultant to the Special Assistant to the President on Science
and Technology; Consultant to the U.S. Senate Subcommittee on National Policy
Machinery; and Staff Director of the OECD Advisory Group on Science Policy.

names. Let me suggest what that was, and leave aside what we
call it.

What we both saw was a new need that Alvin Weinberg has,
I think, described well in his 1963 White House report, *Science,
Government, and Information.* I remind you, briefly, of what he
said:

> Retrieval of documents is not the same as retrieval of infor-
> mation; a technical specialist really needs the information
> contained in the published literature, not the published litera-
> ture itself. To retrieve information, as contrasted to docu-
> ments, the technical community has devised the specialized
> data and information center.
>
> . . . .
>
> Specialized information centers, to be fully effective, must
> be operated in closest possible contact with working scientists
> and engineers in the field. The activities of the most success-
> ful centers are an intrinsic part of science and technology.
> The centers not only disseminate and retrieve information;
> they create new information. . . . The process of sifting through
> large masses of data often leads to new generalizations. . . .
> Knowledgeable scientific interpreters who can collect relevant
> data, review a field, and distill information in a manner that
> goes to the heart of a technical situation are more help to the
> overburdened specialist than is a mere pile of relevant docu-
> ments . . . they make an information center a technical institute
> rather than a technical library.[1]

Two points should be noted in passing. First, in the passage I
have quoted, Weinberg is of course talking specifically about the
information needs of scientists and engineers, but I gather it should
not be difficult to extend the idea to professionals of other disciplines investigating other subject matters.

Second, Weinberg does not propose the specialized information
center as a substitute or replacement for the enterprise of collecting, cataloging, and retrieving books and documents. Rather is it
"backed by large central depositories. . . . Its input is the output of
the central depository." But that, however important, is no longer
very interesting. The problems of documentation, thanks to

[1] U.S. President's Science Advisory Committee, *Science, Government, and
Information: The Responsibilities of the Technical Community and the Gov-
ernment in the Transfer of Information; a Report* (Washington, D.C.: Govt.
Print. Off., 1963), p.32-33.

pioneer work already done, are by now much more technical than intellectual.

What is interesting, I think, is that all such schemes as that proposed by Weinberg depend on the ability of the people involved, not to act merely as passive communication or transmission belts, but to collect, assimilate, and, above all, to transform information for new uses. Genuine communication, as many students of the subject have often noted, is creative of something new.

My mandate for today, in a rather pretentious phrase for which I respectfully disclaim responsibility, is to talk about the "intellectual implications" in the current dialogue about the "Present Status and Future Prospects of Reference/Information Work." I shall try to be responsive to the mandate by telling you about a conference I participated in recently and by saying something further concerning my own information problems at Harvard, about which Doug Bryant and I have been conferring. Both, I think, point to some of the new intellectual needs with which new proposals such as Weinberg's are trying to grapple.

The conference was about the impact of computers and information technology on industrial management. One of the specific questions was: "Has the advent of computers altered the function or organization of the top management of a company? And if so, how?" The discussion ranged over the whole spectrum of (1) what managers do; (2) how they do it; (3) the relation of information, authority, and responsibility; (4) whether machines can think; and (5) the nature of and distinction among policy making, planning, and implementation of directives.

To everyone's surprise, something of a consensus emerged. It was that computers do not change the function of top management but they do change its organization. I shall rehearse briefly the logic of the consensus, because I think it has a direct bearing on what interests us here today.

There is, as you know, serious disagreement among logicians and computer experts about whether the more and more complex and sophisticated computers that are being developed will ever be able to think. Certainly, they already calculate, infer, and search out proofs of geometrical theorems far better than most people do; but, the question goes, can they really think? The answer hinges on whether thinking is a process that is completely describable. Even the most bullish partisan of the computer has never claimed more than that the computer can in principle simulate any activity that can be described completely, that is, that can be rendered completely in linguistic form.

The conclusion of the conference that the function of management was not affected by the computer hinged on agreement by the

participants that the most essential function of management is prelinguistic: it is made up of such things as perception, intuition,
sensitivity, and courage. These are activities that cannot be completely described in language, and they are therefore not subject to
performance by computers, even in principle. Actual flesh-and-
blood managers, of course, engage in activities that are a mixture
of both the linguistic and the prelinguistic. Until perfect computers are developed, in other words, the manager and his staff
still have to do "computer-type" work. They have to receive, assemble, and analyze information and discover the conclusions to
which it points. Their numbers and organization must, therefore,
be such as to enable them to do this. But since information is by
definition something that is or can be put into linguistic form,
there is a presumption that computers will someday take over the
job of receiving, assembling, analyzing, and inferring from it. Then
the manager will be free to concentrate all of his attention on the
nonlinguistic, the ineffable, parts of his job. He may reduce his staff,
fire his middle-level managers, and otherwise reorganize himself
into a man-machine system, but he will not be less of a top manager for all that; if anything, he will be more so.

This analysis receives unexpected support from another quarter. I recall to you the geometry that all of us learned in high
school. I ask you to conceive of it as a language—a language that
makes statements about lines, and triangles, and squares, and all
that. Now you will, I am sure, remember that all the statements
in that language—all the theorems, we called them—were derivable
from five postulates, which were given, by means of a small number
of rules that specified how the derivations should be made. The postulates and the rules together gave what I have called "a complete description" of the language of geometry; and, sure enough, there are
computers today that do geometry far better than I ever could.

Remember also, however, that there was a geometry teacher
who made statements about geometry. He made such statements
as: "There are five postulates"; "One of these is the postulate
about parallel lines"; "Plane geometry deals in only two dimensions"; "Its vocabulary consists of points and lines"; and so
forth. Now these statements are not statements of the language
of geometry; they are not themselves theorems. They are
about the language of geometry. They are themselves statements in another language—English, we call it. And English, as is
evident enough, is *not* completely described. We cannot infer all
of the statements or propositions in it from a fixed set of known
postulates by a small number of derivation or transformation
rules. Because English is a language, it *could* be, in principle,
completely described; but the point is that you would then have to

use still another language to do the describing. In the past decades, logicians have shown that, for every fully described language,
there is another language that you use for the description that cannot itself be fully described.

Every fully described language can be fed into a computer.
When they have been, there remains the language of the program-
mer who does the feeding, just as top management remains to
do the prelinguistic job even after all the information handling
is done for him by machine.

Now, please bear with me while I try to illustrate a very analogous point in a much less technical context—that of our program
at Harvard. When I arrived at Harvard at the beginning of the program, about a year and a half ago, my colleagues and I were told,
in effect, something like the following: "Here are $5 million, ten
years, any intellectual resources you can tap, and a title—Technology and Society. Do something!" The title, as you might guess,
gave us far more difficulty than any of the other components. The
rubric is so broad that anything could be justified under it; therefore, our problem from the start has been much less what to include than what to exclude. It would have been too easy to adopt a
simple foundation approach and support a number of individually
worthwhile projects, only to wind up with discrete findings that did
not add up to illumination of any larger questions.

We decided, therefore, to start with the questions. We took a
leaf from an eminent thinker at Columbia University, my teacher
and friend, John Herman Randall, Jr., who has said:

> Above all ... come questions. Questions really determine ...
> the resulting answers: the "meaning" of the answers or
> statements depends on the prior questions to which they are
> answers ... and their function or "meaning" is ultimately
> ascertainable only as the answers to specific questions.[2]

We therefore decided to tackle first the question, "What are
the major questions that a program on technology and society
should be asking?," and to devote our major effort during the first
years to identifying and formulating those major questions. Only
then would we start systematic and large-scale inquiry into answers.

The mechanisms we are employing to formulate our questions
are what are often called interdisciplinary. We have a study
group which meets one afternoon a week. It is made up of a

---

[2] John Herman Randall, Jr., "The Art of Language and the Linguistic Situation: A Naturalistic Analysis," *Journal of Philosophy*, 60:42-43 (Jan. 3, 1963).

mathematician and computer expert, a sociologist, an economist, a philosopher, a historian, and a professor each from the Business School and the School of Education. We try, in this group, first to learn to communicate with one another and then to cut through to the questions that the program should be asking.

We also have two interdisciplinary research groups on particular subjects. Our computer expert, a learning psychologist, and a public school superintendent are trying to identify the implications of information technology for the schooling process at the secondary level. A historian of science, a medical doctor, a biologist, and possibly a theologian will soon be investigating the social, political, and ethical issues potential in soon-to-be-expected breakthroughs in biomedical technology. And so it goes.

That is the context of our information needs. What I hope I have evoked for you is that we are engaged in an enterprise that, for the moment, is less one of research than of thinking, if I might make that distinction. The difference, in the terms I have suggested already, is that research is concerned with finding answers, whereas thinking, at least when narrowly defined, is concerned more, if I may so put it, with finding questions.

Libraries, traditionally, have been concerned with finding answers. So, by and large, have reference services. They have been, are, and will in some form continue to be indispensable aids to research. The new need is for a comparable aid to thinking; and it is to this need that I and, I think, Alvin Weinberg are seeking to address ourselves.

You might ask, "What is so new about thinking?" It has been done, and not indifferently, since long before Aristotle. But let us examine Aristotle. He had command of all the knowledge there was. He was his time's leading physicist, biologist, psychologist, political scientist, art critic, logician, philosopher, and theologian. He was not preeminent in history and geometry, but there is fairly good evidence that he was not entirely unfamiliar with those fields either, if only as a rather talented student.

With this equipment, Aristotle formulated a metaphysics and a theology that summed up his world in ways that made sense of the whole and gave it meaning. He did original research in his individual areas of competence, and then put his findings together into new syntheses, into new insights and new ideas. That is, he used his particular knowledge of particular fields as equipment for thinking, in the distinctive, synthetic, innovative sense of the term. He was a one-man interdisciplinary team, if you wish.

No one today can have command of all the knowledge of his time. The most that anyone can hope for is command of a special discipline. But what one does in a special discipline is research—

more and more digging for more and more answers to essentially
the same set of questions. The bud of thinking, to vary the meta-
phor, gets lost in the bush of research. As I have said elsewhere,
"There is a distressing frequency of peripheral and subcritical
inquiries that are always 'preparing the ground' for understanding
of the big questions, and [a] relative rarity of attempts to do the
actual understanding."

This is what gives rise to all the talk about team research,
about interdisciplinary thinking or cross-disciplinary dialogue,
and about systems analysis or the systems approach to problem
solving. Many account such ideas as new, unproved, and therefore
lacking in respectability. Yet are they so new as all that? Aristotle, as I have tried to show, must be accounted the prime example of genuine interdisciplinary thinking. What is new is that
interdisciplinary thinking—just plain thinking is the traditional
name for it—can no longer be done by single persons. Single persons do research and solve problems; but they are increasingly
prevented, by the sheer mass of knowledge, from achieving the
kind of intellectual syntheses that are, in the end, the essence of
thinking.

The essence of thinking is like the rules that govern a geometric system and like the function of top management. It is, in
each case, the part that is not completely describable because it is
creative of the new: new ideas and new questions; new postulates
and derivation rules; new "hunches" about how to act after all the
information is in.

Thinking, I have suggested, can no longer be done wholly in a
single head. And, as soon as you try to do it with many heads, you
raise the problem of communication among those heads. In our
study group, mentioned earlier, we are always asking one another
—the seven or eight of us—what sociologists have said about this,
or economists about that, or mathematicians about the other, and
historians and philosophers and educators about the rest. Who is
doing what thinking that might help with the problem we are trying
to define? Are we sure we are aware of what is being done on this
question elsewhere, in this country and abroad? Are there ideas,
or articles, or books that might illuminate it, even though their own
intent is ostensibly different?

It is questions such as these, I am suggesting, that define the
new role of the information specialist. The nature of intellectual
work is shifting significantly to thinking anew about the problems
of our age, to starting once more, if you wish, on the search for
wisdom rather than on the search just for knowledge. Knowledge
can be dug out of laboratories and books and libraries. Wisdom
has to be created; and it will be created out of the mass of

accumulated knowledge that is now too great for one or a few to grasp, and that we must rely on a new breed of collators, reviewers, compilers, abstracters, bibliographers, sifters, and distillers to collect and prepare and cook into acceptable food for thought.

Library jobs that are completely describable are like factory jobs that are completely describable. Machines, as they realize their full potential, will take these jobs over increasingly from people who have, up to now, had to function as machines because the machines have not up to now been there. That may not be tomorrow; but it will be soon.

The new breed of servants of learning, necessary to the new problems of learning that I have been describing, by contrast are, in Weinberg's phrase, a group of "dedicated and knowledgeable technical men who help interpret and assimilate the literature for others working in the field." They are not librarians in any antiquated sense, which was the allusion of my opening remark. They are, rather, what Doug Bryant called the "good librarians" that scholars and thinkers increasingly need and must have.

Comment

Grieg Aspnes

Our keynote for this session was struck when it was stated that reference/information service is the essence of all librarianship. From that, we can go on to say that the heart of reference or information service is the index. This is the key that unlocks the treasures of man's recorded knowledge, ideas, and experiences.

If money were no object, a library could have one person in charge of each book or each chapter of each book, every article of every magazine, and every report or every part of every report. To search this collection, you would only have to call out, "Has anyone the answer to this question or any information relating to it?" Whoever had it (being perfectly familiar with what he had) would push a button, light a light, or sing out, "I have it."

But money is an object, a very important object, and it is one part of the basic problem of reference/information service that the new methods of information retrieval are trying to solve. The other part is our struggle to devise a system that will tell us more precisely, more quickly, and more easily what thoughts, ideas, and experiences we have in our collection of graphic records. This is an intellectual problem which reference service has never in the past solved adequately. The problem is compounded now by the increased size and complexity of the stored material and by the tremendously increased need for a better information service.

We need to ask some basic questions. Is it better to catalog

Grieg Aspnes, Research Librarian, Cargill, Incorporated, Minneapolis, has served as President of the Special Libraries Association and has taught courses in special librarianship at the library school of the University of Minnesota. He is the author of "The Current Situation in Documentation" in the *Bowker Annual of Library and Book Trade Information*, 1962-1965 inclusive.

or index a few items ideally and completely, or will we be able to provide better reference service from a larger store of less perfectly indexed materials?

Sanford and Stiles suggested that "the world's libraries are monuments of over-processed and over-catalogued trivia and under-processed and under-catalogued vital information, for the obvious reason that the Catalog Department expended much the same effort on each."[1]

We also need to ask some questions about the validity of the indexes on which we depend. This probes the very nature of what an index is supposed to do and how well it is doing it. The research of Cleverdon in England is merely a beginning. Comparing the relative efficiency of various types of indexes on the basis of "recall and relevance" may be a snare and a delusion. Who can decide whether an index has found what is needed? Only the user; only the person who needs the information and knows whether the information found satisfies his need. Even so, he cannot assess the quantity and value of relevant information which he has failed to discover.

We need, therefore, to take a new look at the library user, his needs, his habits, his attitudes. No one can claim that everyone who needs information is getting all he needs; we cannot even claim that everyone who needs information is asking for it. Why not? We need more studies like that of Hanson, who found that the library was the last place to which a large group of researchers turned when they needed information.[2] Why? And what can we do about it?

The ultimate theoretical (and practical) goal of any reference library or information center must be to supply its users with all the information, and only the information, they need, at the lowest possible cost. Or, to use the popular phrase, "the right information to the right person at the right time in the right form."

A quotation from Weinberg is appropriate here:

The whole spirit and tradition of librarianship has been dominated by the notion that the librarian's primary task is to connect the user with documents that may contain the information he is seeking. Document retrieval is a prerequisite to

---

[1] J. Albert Sanford and H. Edmund Stiles, "The Principle of Minimum Control," in American Documentation Institute, *Parameters of Information Science;* proceedings of the 1964 Annual Meeting of the American Documentation Institute, Philadelphia, October 5-8, 1964 (Washington, D.C.: A.D.I., ₍c1964₎), 1:425-26.

[2] C. W. Hanson, "Research on Users' Needs: Where Is It Getting Us?" *Aslib Proceedings,* 16:64-75 (Feb., 1964).

information retrieval—but it is only a prerequisite: an information system that stops short of transferring information
from one human mind to another is inadequate.[3]

This is a basic and primary responsibility of all reference librarians. Asking these questions about ourselves, about our systems, about our performance, and about our users' needs and
satisfactions is also our responsibility. Perhaps for the first time
in the history of librarianship, these problems are being examined
on a scientific research basis. We have a long way to go. Dr.
Mesthene talked today about the importance of thinking about a
problem, of defining it, and of asking questions. Joseph Becker
mentioned some of the machinery and methods now being tried and
studied for solutions to some parts of our problems. We reference
librarians have to look both ways. We have to keep in touch with
the deep thinkers and do some deep thinking ourselves and, at the
same time, watch the development and testing of new machines,
methods, techniques, and systems, while back at the reference
desk our customers still clamor for information service.
The coming of automation, mechanization, and data-processing
equipment has forced the librarian to do systems analysis and to
make intensive studies of all the important elements that help supply information and graphic records to the user. There can be no
question but that machines are finding important places in the library. A more important question is how we can induce more patrons to use the library and how we can better satisfy their needs.
The basic challenge to reference/information service is to offer
the kind of service that:

1. Produces the information necessary to satisfy the request
2. Provides it quickly, in some cases even before it is requested
3. Provides it accurately, specifically, selectively, completely,
but in the briefest, most easily usable form
4. Provides it from a variety of sources (not only the conventional printed sources, but from near-print, government and
other institutional reports, convention proceedings, symposia, foreign-language publications, and other media); and
5. Provides it with evaluative discrimination, suited to the
needs of the user.

---

[3] Alvin M. Weinberg, "Scientific Communication," *International Science
and Technology*, 16:67 (Apr., 1963).

Discussion

Aspnes: I would like to ask Dr. Mesthene whether the computer can think. When one cannot tell whether a human or a machine is providing the information and responding to questions, is the machine thinking?

Mesthene: It depends on what the communication is about. If it is about things completely describable in language, then I might wonder what was at the other end of the teletype, whether it was a machine, or a man functioning as a machine. I would start worrying if the machine started painting pictures or composing string quartets.

Reynolds: What is wrong with the machine thinking?

Mesthene: I should not be interpreted as having said that I am upset by the prospect that machines might think. Whether they think or not is a relatively idle question. What you want is to distinguish the analytic from the creative. I would argue that machines, in principle, are very adept at the analytic and probably, in principle, not adept at the creative.

Carnovsky: Dr. Mesthene, I was interested in your distinction between wisdom and knowledge, and particularly between finding answers and raising the right questions. I wonder if you would tell us a little about the kind of questions that your group is raising. Are they philosophical questions about the nature of the good life or the nature of God, or just what are they?

Mesthene: I tried to indicate some of them by describing two research groups that we have under way. One group is trying to answer the question: what are the implications of computer technology, both existing and potential, for the process of schooling? Perhaps I will say a word more about that to indicate what it contains, what the thinking behind it is. This

168

group is going to spend, roughly, one academic year on this as
a start. They will spend about the first half of the year con-
structing a model of what the schooling process would look
like if you cranked in all of the available computer technology:
what this technology does to the teacher, to the teacher's
training, to the teacher's qualifications and attitudes, to the
teacher-student relationship, to the differential rates of learning of the students, to grading methods and the effects of grading, to the grading profile or the achievement profile that goes
into the employment application, to family life if you should wind
up with an on-line computer in every home, to the school building if it needs change. About the middle of the year, after they
have created this Orwellian monster, we would expect them to
step back and ask whether we want it. What would be the implications of such a schooling system for some of the major
educational issues and controversies that are presently under
discussion?

The other group, which is working on biomedical technology, is much less well defined, because we are much less well
prepared to conceive what form social, political, and ethical
questions will take when it is in man's power to replace a
heart or a liver when his own gives out, and, above all, when it
is in man's power to achieve what was first prognosticated in
Plato's *Republic*—the possibility of breeding exactly the kinds
of human beings that are wanted. The thing that is—I am
struggling between the words "alarming" and "encouraging"—
about this (I'll leave the ambiguity) is that these possibilities
are much closer than we think, according to some of the people
who, I suppose, should know best. The time when these technologies will be realities is probably not more than twenty
years away. What we are trying to do is, at least, to mark out
the channels along which people had better start thinking
about how they are going to handle these problems when
they arise.

That is on one end of the spectrum. On the other end of
the spectrum, inevitably, is that everything we talk about and
think about is going to get us into the problem of values: re-
ligious values, or philosophical values, or ethical values. We
are going to take our time about that one. There are many
people talking about this, and very few of them are saying anything, and we do not want just to join the chorus. We would
like first to get some handle on it, to feel that we can
come up with some slightly more concrete, slightly more
operationally useful propositions, before we go into the value
question.

Adams: In reference to Dr. Mesthene's comment about the use of
    interdisciplinary mechanisms, is there, in fact, any categori-
    zation of knowledge that exists today that we can truly call a
    discipline in the classic sense? And, if there is, how do you
    define it?

Mesthene: There is at least one—academic economics.

Reynolds: Mr. Aspnes, what is wrong with the library being the
    last place consulted?

Aspnes: ... I am convinced that the library should be the *first*
    place, if it is properly performing its responsibilities. If it is
    a true information center, it should be the best place to start a
    systematic search for whatever has been recorded anywhere,
    in any language, that relates to the problem the person wants
    answered. Our goal is to save the time of the person who
    might wander a long time looking for information that could
    be found for him more quickly and more efficiently by a
    reference/information center.

Freiser: I am in agreement with much of what you say, Mr.
    Aspnes, but I find it difficult to understand why you continue
    to use the word "index" to designate the heart of library ser-
    vice. I know that you are equating "index" with: how do we
    find out? or, how do we retrieve? But this word also seems
    to imply that a lot of information is printed information, verbal
    information, and is available in bibliographic sources. It would
    seem to me that the heart of the problem is not how we have
    access to printed information, but: what is information; are
    there other means of access; is there a man-computer rela-
    tionship which may develop about which we do not know enough
    today, which may cause the word "index," as we know it today,
    to disappear?

Aspnes: Strictly speaking, an index points to something, doesn't it?
    An index to infrared spectra consists of red squiggles on a
    piece of paper. It is a record, but not in words. You are right
    that information can take many forms—heartbeats are infor-
    mation—and we do deal in many forms of information. ... I
    use the word "index" to mean an indicator of any kind or form
    that points to sources of information.

Question: (What will the computer mean to the small or average-
    sized library?)

Dubester: There seems to be a notion that every library is going
    to automate; it must get a computer, the computer will be pro-
    grammed, and somehow you are going to put questions into that
    computer and answers will come back. I think that this is not
    the way things are going to happen at all. Today, the Bell tele-
    phone network is transmitting more data than voice on its

channels. The problem of access to computers is going to be
resolved by our being able to communicate with a computer
just by picking up the telephone. At Lehigh University, access
to the computer at the University of Pennsylvania is being considered. A computer utility will have the problem of all other
utilities; but it will be part of our social fabric, and everybody
will have access to it relatively cheaply. At that point, we will
communicate just the way we normally do today with data
links, except that we will be using a system that is programmed, very explicit, very rigorous, and involving a lot of
constraints to which one must adapt.

Hayes: We have tended to forget that some segments of our communities do not yet even know what reference service is. Mr.
Lorenz briefly touched on legislation; but we did not pick this
up in terms of describing the kind of systems that are developing in less-populated areas, where a communications center
and a network mean nothing at all. You cannot talk in terms of
tapping in by a telephone line to a poverty-stricken Sioux Indian on the Rosebud Reservation in South Dakota.

I want to carry Mr. Freiser's discussion of a reference
resource center a little further. I have a feeling that, in addition to describing the librarian's relationship to the cultural
life of our communities—to recreation, to music, to the arts—
somehow we have to tie ourselves in with certain other information givers in a community. Again, maybe I am thinking too
much in terms of a widely scattered population area, a rural
community. But what about relating the information center to
the services of the extension agent, the health officer, the pro-
bation officer?

Dubester: I think Miss Hayes is suggesting that there is a difference between the means, the mechanisms, and the overall
social system in which a library operates—that there is a
broader framework within which some of these developments
have to be viewed, measured, and assessed, and that this is
relatively difficult because it is a multiple rather than a single
factor framework.

Implications for the Future of Reference/Information Service

Frederick G. Kilgour

For a historian, the clearest view of the future is gained by the examination of developments in the past. Thereby, one discovers the path which has brought us to the present situation, delineates and evaluates the present position, and from such a base extrapolates into the future. However, the randomness that prevents human history from being deterministic dims the view as years are stretched out ahead. Therefore, when this paper peers forward, it will look to the foreseeable future, which, due to dynamic developments in machining of information, can be here in but a half-dozen years.

THE PAST

In the two decades from 1840 to 1860, the United States experienced a remarkable awakening of intellectual activity in the arts, literature, scholarship, and the sciences.[1] This activity spread among the populace as a whole; it promoted the establishment of new subscription libraries and, toward the end of the period, the initiation of the modern public library movement. It also stimulated reading and the use of books and libraries and was

---

Frederick G. Kilgour, Associate Librarian for Research and Development, Yale University Library since 1965, was formerly librarian of the Yale Medical Library. Mr. Kilgour teaches the history of American science and the history of technology; his articles have appeared in medical, scientific, technical, and library periodicals and in proceedings of institutes and conferences.

▶ [1] Robert E. Riegel, *Young America, 1830-1840* (Norman, Okla.: Univ. of Oklahoma Pr., 1949); Carl R. Fish, *The Rise of the Common Man* ("A History of American Life," v. 6 [New York: Macmillan, 1927]).

unquestionably the major force that turned the attention of librarians to the invention of reference aids. Over the millennia that separated the ancient library at Alexandria from the libraries of the 1840's, librarians had been custodians, collectors, and catalogers. Now they were to add the function of use to their collections.

Presumably, librarians have always helped users to locate information in volumes under their custody, but it was not until the 1840's that librarians began to devise special tools to aid users. Perhaps the first important new type of reference tool was Charles Coffin Jewett's use of specific subject entries in the construction of a subject index to the catalog of the Brown University Library that he published in 1843.[2] Charles Ammi Cutter subsequently remarked that "Mr. Jewett was thinking more about those who are seeking information than those who are searching for a book."[3] His specific subject entries had the important characteristic of being able to be interfiled among author and title entries. William Frederick Poole employed this method in his catalog of the Boston Mercantile Library[4] of 1854, which was the forerunner of the modern dictionary catalog. Jewett brought the use of subject headings to the modern level in the 1858 subject index to a catalog of the Boston Public Library.[5]

Poole had also produced the first index to articles and magazines in 1848.[6] This publication proved to be the forebear of all subsequent journal indexes. Apparently, from the time Poole first worked in one of the Yale collegiate libraries in the 1840's, he was devoted to servicing users and never viewed librarianship as a purely custodial activity. When he became librarian of the Chicago Public Library in 1874, he established a separate reference collection, and he encouraged readers to come into his office to seek assistance. Although he encouraged readers to come in and left

[2] Brown University, Library, *A Catalogue of the Library of Brown University, in Providence, Rhode Island, with an Index of Subjects* (Providence, 1843).

[3] U.S. Bureau of Education, *Public Libraries in the United States of America, Their History, Condition, and Management* (Dept. of the Interior, Bureau of Education, Special Report, Part I [Washington, D.C.: Govt. Print. Off., 1876]), p.539.

[4] Boston, Mercantile Library Association, *Catalogue of the Mercantile Library of Boston* (Boston: J. Wilson and Son, 1854).

[5] Boston Public Library, *Index to the Catalogue of a Portion of the Public Library of the City of Boston, Arranged in the Lower Hall* (Boston: G. C. Rand and Avery, 1858).

[6] [Poole's Index to Periodical Literature], *An Alphabetical Index to Subjects Treated in the Reviews, and Other Periodicals* ... (New York: G. P. Putnam, 1848).

the door open, he did not encourage them to stay, for over that door was a sign reading, "Be Short."[7]

While Poole was helping readers in Chicago, Samuel S. Green in Worcester, Massachusetts, was also giving his attention to the needs of patrons. The first volume of the *Library Journal*, which appeared in 1876, published his paper entitled "Personal Relations between Librarians and Readers."[8] This paper attracted wide attention. Indeed, newspapers in Boston commented on the advanced services available at Worcester but lacking in their own library.

A second important development in intellectual activity occurred in the 1870's and 1880's, for it was during this period that American colleges began to give graduate instruction and to evolve into universities. To be sure, Yale had granted the first earned American Ph.D.'s in 1861, but not until the 1870-1890 era did graduate education begin to flourish. The new graduate teaching emphasized training the student to design and carry out research programs independently, so that he could be not only an effective college teacher but also a productive scholar who would, in turn, lead young students in graduate training. The new graduate education was to have an immediate and continuing impact on libraries.

In the memorable year 1876, Melvil Dewey, then at Amherst College, published the first edition of his *Classification and Subject Index*, which initiated the important transition from broad to specific classification, although "the system was devised for cataloguing and indexing purposes."[9] Dewey's decimal classification and the subsequent Library of Congress classification are valuable tools for reference librarians. Therefore, a narrow classification scheme, subject catalogs, and journal indexes—indispensable reference tools—were in existence by 1876.

However, it was not until 1884 that the profession of reference librarian was born. In that never-to-be-forgotten year, Dewey appointed two full-time reference assistants to the Columbia University Library Reference Room. These two gentlemen, George Baker and William G. Baker, are the heroic pioneers of reference librarianship.[10]

---

[7] William L. Williamson, *William Frederick Poole and the Modern Library Movement* (New York: Columbia Univ. Pr., 1963), p.120.

[8] Samuel S. Green, "Personal Relations between Librarians and Readers," *Library Journal*, 1:74-81 (Nov. 30, 1876).

[9] [Melvil Dewey], *A Classification and Subject Index for Cataloguing and Arranging the Books and Pamphlets of a Library* (Amherst, Mass.: 1876), p.[3].

[10] Samuel Rothstein, *The Development of Reference Services through Academic Traditions, Public Library Practice and Special Librarianship* ("ACRL Monographs," No. 14 [Chicago: Association of College and Reference Libraries, 1955]), p.28.

By 1900, the full-time position of reference assistant in public and university libraries was well established, but it required another third of a century before libraries were giving reference service on a broad base. For instance, it was not until the later 1930's that the Harvard College Library had a librarian on the reference staff assigned to helping undergraduates.

During the period up to World War II, there were two major viewpoints in giving reference service. The older view held that the user should be given aid in using the library so that he could find his own information, while the newer view was that the library staff should actually find the information needed by the user. This second view was embodied in the establishment of information centers, largely in scientific and industrial libraries. Perhaps the principal characteristic of a scientific or technical information center was that the staff could prepare a state-of-the-art paper on a scientific or technical topic when asked to do so. In more classical librarianship, there was Thomas P. Fleming's important early innovation at the Columbia Medical Library—a continuous bibliographic service[11] which preceded by a quarter of a century the dissemination of selected information techniques now being developed on computers.

Following World War II, libraries and information centers continued to develop along lines laid out in the 1920's and 1930's. There was an amazing expansion in numbers of special libraries, associated with the expansion in research activities in universities, industry, and commerce. However, for the most part, the situation was essentially that of 1884. There were specialized staff members to help users, and the major reference tools were the subject catalog of books, subject classification of books on the shelves, and indexes to journal articles.

THE PRESENT

There are three major developments at the present time which will determine the future of reference and information services. First, there is the remarkable expansion of the "knowledge industry"; second, the invention of that remarkable information-processing machine, the electronic digital computer, and its

---

[11] Thomas P. Fleming, "Medical Library," in Columbia University, College of Physicians and Surgeons, *Report of the Dean* . . . (June 30, 1940), p.64-66; Thomas P. Fleming, Estelle Brodman, and Seymour Robb, "A Continuous Bibliography Service in University Libraries," *College and Research Libraries*, 8:322-28 (July, 1947).

application to libraries; third, the introduction of systems concepts
and systems thinking into libraries.

The first major intellectual development affecting reference
and information work is the current explosion of the so-called
"knowledge industry," which is a not entirely anticipated development from graduate education. In 1962 Fritz Machlup reported
that 29 percent of the gross national product of the United States in
1958 was due to the knowledge industry.[12] In the next year, Clark
Kerr predicted that the knowledge industry would be the focal point
of American economic development in the second half of the twentieth century, just as the automobile industry had been the focal
point in the first half of the century and the railroad industry in
the last half of the nineteenth.[13] More recently, James A. Perkins
has discussed "the explosive power of knowledge" and its impact
on universities and society.[14]

As a result of the growth of this new industry, knowledge and
information have assumed a central position in our society during
the last decade, and it has been this shift which has generated new
demands on libraries. In other words, libraries now find themselves in a central and responsible position in society which is
quite unlike their status in the millennia of their previous existence. The new and urgent demands on libraries for information
are forcing them to become more flexible institutions.

Perhaps the most fruitful picture a librarian can have of a
computer is of an information-processing machine or a symbol
manipulator. Actually, a computer can do only five things: (1) it
can move characters; (2) it can compare characters; (3) it can relate characters; (4) it can make simple yes-no decisions; and (5) it
can add. Libraries can take advantage of the first four capabilities.
However, it should also be mentioned that the computer has the remarkable characteristic of being able to take in and store instructions as to how it should manipulate symbols subsequently read into
it. Such programs are limitless in variety, and it is this ability of
the computer to replace in its memory a limitless number of sets
of instructions that gives it its fantastic flexibility in information
processing.

Initial library applications of computers have been concerned
with the mechanization of library procedures and with bibliographic
information retrieval. Computers have been employed in the

---

[12] Fritz Machlup, *The Production and Distribution of Knowledge in the
United States* (Princeton: Princeton Univ. Pr., 1962), p.362.

[13] Clark Kerr, *The Uses of the University* (Cambridge: Harvard Univ. Pr.,
1963), p.88.

[14] James A. Perkins, *The University in Transition* (Princeton: Princeton
Univ. Pr., 1966).

mechanization of circulation records, serial records, cataloging procedures, and technical processing. In addition, management information systems have been imposed on these computerized processes so that library managers can now obtain information about library processing hitherto unavailable. However, some computer applications have been unhappy because mechanization has been carried out without reference to the fact that a library is a total system. Whenever a procedure is mechanized without also being planned to be compatible with other library mechanization, it will be necessary to redo the computerization at some future date.

While mechanization of library procedures in essence mechanizes, and relieves the staff of, simple, repetitive routines, the computerization of bibliographic information retrieval computerizes the user. The link between bibliographic information retrieval and library mechanization is through cataloging and indexing, which are clearly the central processes. Two of the best-known bibliographic information retrievals are the MEDLARS system of the National Library of Medicine,[15] which is a sequential search for information on tapes, and the on-line retrieval system of the Lockheed Missiles and Space Company, which is an extraordinarily rapid search in a random-access file of bibliographic information.[16] The principal contributions of computers to library information processing are (1) high speed in information processing; (2) flexibility of processing; (3) absolute accuracy; and (4) compatibility of different forms of output from the same record. These remarkable characteristics demand that computer applications be imaginative and not merely the computerization of present procedures.

The third important current development for the future of reference work has been the introduction of systems thinking into library procedures work. Modern systems thinking originated about two decades ago and is characterized by its comprehensive approach, its choice of objectives, and its acceptance of the principle that living or mechanical systems are information systems. Of course, this recognition of library procedures as being information systems is the major difference between the old and the new, but the operation of the new systems would not be possible without computers.

---

[15] Scott Adams, "MEDLARS: Performance, Problems, Possibilities," *Bulletin of the Medical Library Association*, 53:139-51 (Apr. 1965).

[16] D. L. Drew, R. K. Summit, R. I. Tanaka, and R. B. Whiteley, "An Online Technical Library Reference Retrieval System," *American Documentation*, 17:3-7 (Jan., 1966).

A system is often defined as an "ongoing process that yields some desired result," but this definition is not a particularly fruitful one. Nevertheless, it is important to realize that a system is a dynamic process and not a fixed, machine-like procedure like those to which libraries have been accustomed. The application of systems thinking is changing libraries from their former inflexibility into an evolving process, and it is information which is in process.

The comprehensiveness of library systems should not be confined to a single library, for library systems will include regional networks, as well as national networks such as the postal system or the telephone system. Library systems will also include management information systems, for once the principle is accepted that a library system is an information system, it is then obvious that information can be retrieved from the system that delineates the state of the system. This type of information is what a manager needs in the direction of operation of the system.

THE FUTURE

The history of reference and information services over the past century and the current developments in the knowledge industry, computer-library applications, and systems concepts suggest at least five major events in the immediate future which have implications for the evolution of reference and information services: (1) the elaboration of library systems in the new sense of that phrase; (2) studies of users' needs; (3) a rise in library research; (4) imaginative computer applications; and (5) a new intellectual approach in librarianship.

Individual libraries consist of four major subsystems: (1) information store; (2) communications; (3) buildings; and (4) users. The information store consists of two types of information: (1) books, pamphlets, serials, manuscripts, reports, films, records, and pictures; and (2) card catalogs, index and abstract journals, printed catalogs, and bibliographies. A communication subsystem could contain telephones and automobiles; buildings— the library building, other buildings; and grounds. Traditionally, the user has only been considered as a subsystem during the process of library building design, when all four subsystems are treated as an integrated whole, but the design of the catalog and book arrangement do not specifically integrate with the modern user subsystem. Indeed, there has been no major redesign of cataloging and classification processes during the past half century; rather, cataloging and subject classification are currently based on a conglomerate of *a priori* bibliographic, classificatory, and economic principles largely developed in the four decades preceding the first World War. It has been the task of the reference librarian to fit the user to this antiquated information store. The future will see the information store designed to fit the user.

The library networks of the future will also have the user as a subsystem. Today, these networks are not analogous to the postal system but would be analogous to a network of post offices if the originators and recipients of mail were disregarded in the system. Similarly, the present informal library network would be like the telephone system if it were only a network of central exchanges to which each individual would go when he wished to receive a call or transmit a call. In both the actual national postal system and the telephone system, there is emphasis on the user, and an analogous emphasis will be interjected into library system networks of the future.

Extraordinarily little is known of users' needs for information, of the uses of library information, and of the characteristics of users. There have been recent pleas in the literature for the inclusion of the user in library systems, and some of the problems resulting from this inclusion have been pointed out. One of these problems is the difficulty in measuring the productivity of users, and, without doubt, this measurement will be difficult to achieve.[17] However, this anticipated difficulty should not delay consideration of users in library systems.

As soon as users are considered as part of library systems, it is clear that user costs are systems costs. Since it is universally desirable to keep costs at a minimum, it is also clear that efficiency in the user subsystem must be attained. It will not be necessary to do a study of users' needs to know that one objective of the system will be to minimize the amount of time required for a user to obtain either bibliographic or textual information.

Nevertheless, studies of users' information needs are required for a host of purposes related to the design of library systems. At present, there is almost no knowledge available as to how library users employ books and journals and for what purposes they use them. Obviously, there needs to be a detailed understanding of users' needs to define objectives of the library subsystems. Similarly, there is the equivalent need to know how library information is used. Design of library systems will certainly vary depending on whether college professors use books, as opposed to journals, largely for the preparation of lectures or to infuse new ideas into their research programs. At present, no one knows how professors use books.

---

[17] Edwin B. Parker, "The User's Place in an Information System," *American Documentation*, 17:26-27 (Jan., 1966).

The study of users' characteristics, users' needs, and the use
of library information is a huge research program in itself, but
research on these library unknowns, so to speak, has begun to
produce useful results. Until the present, library knowledge has
been empirical knowledge. It has been knowledge acquired from
experience, literally over centuries. And, as is typical of such
knowledge, its acquisition has been usually unexpected and on a
hit-or-miss basis. An immense corpus of knowledge can be acquired by this empirical technique over long periods of time, but
its acquisition is a desperately slow and unplanned process. With
the advent of new demands on libraries, it has become necessary
for libraries to evolve more rapidly than they have at any time in
the past, but the evolution should be well planned and well directed.
To achieve these desiderata, it will be necessary to have much
more effective information available and to develop that information rapidly. It was in the natural sciences that the extraordinary
efficiency of the research technique for the development of new
knowledge was first demonstrated, in the sixteenth and seventeenth
centuries. Since then, the "scientific method" has pervaded many
areas of investigation and application. It is now time for librarianship to adopt research methods and for librarians to be trained
to do research and to understand the research process and its
products.

Faculties of library schools will be developing research programs analogous to those their scientific colleagues have been
prosecuting for the past century. Research and development
groups will become part of library organizations; at least, they
will be separate organizational units in larger libraries. One of
the major new functions of library schools will be the production
of graduate students to do research and development in libraries.
Although the Graduate Library School at the University of Chicago
has been producing Ph.D.'s in librarianship for several decades,
most of these men and women have become executive librarians
and have not pursued full-time research programs. This condition
will alter in the immediate future so that the recipients of Ph.D.'s
in librarianship will go on in the research and development program instead of in administration.

Of equal importance to training young men and women to do
research will be the training of both young and old to understand
the research process and its products. Of course, library schools
should educate the young in the tactics and strategy of research,
so that each student will assume the burden of pursuing his own
education throughout his professional lifetime.

Older members of the profession must become "do-it-yourself
jailbirds," in the words of John W. Gardner, who points out in

his helpful book, *Self-Renewal,* that "by their mid-thirties most
will have stopped acquiring new skills or new attitudes in any central aspect of their lives."[18]   It is his contention that most individuals have their own intricately designed and self-constructed inner
prisons which block capacity for self-renewal. But, in the years
that lie immediately ahead in librarianship, there will be extensive
need for self-renewal.

Computer applications in the foreseeable future will most
certainly include increasing numbers of computerized stores of
bibliographic information. That is to say, reference librarians
can look forward to working with computerized catalogs and indexes through consoles which may be typewriters or a combination
of a typewriter and a cathode-ray tube. Such a mechanical arrangement will enable the reference assistant to converse with the
computerized catalog at high speeds. His searches for cataloging
and indexing information will be immensely accelerated.

Other products of computer applications will be lists of references, special bibliographies, and some retrieval of factual information. However, in the immediate future, it is unlikely that basic
approaches to literature via author, title, and subject will be
drastically changed.

Reference assistants can also look forward to working with
computer-produced card catalogs, bookform catalogs, and journal
indexes, in addition to consoles. The console approach to bibliographic stores will open up extensive new approaches by subject to
cataloging and indexing information. For instance, catalogers in
the Yale Medical Library have been assigning 10.4 subject headings to each book, these subject headings to be used in a real-time
bibliographic information retrieval system, whereas libraries appear to average about 1.7 subject headings per title.[19]   In other
words, a reference librarian now has 1.7 subject accesses to each
book. However, the simple formula for computing the number of
accesses in an unprecoordinated subject heading system is 2^n-1.[20]
In other words, in a system averaging ten subject headings, the
accesses would be 2^9, or 512. There is no theory or experience
that predicts what the effect of 512 subject accesses will be relative to 1.7. Only from using and doing research on the use of a

---

[18] John W. Gardner, *Self-Renewal* (New York: Harper, ₍c1964₎), p.9.

[19] Frederick G. Kilgour, "Development of Computerization of Card Catalogs in Medical and Scientific Libraries," in Clinic on Library Applications
of Data Processing, University of Illinois, Urbana, 1964, *Proceedings of the
1964 Clinic;* held at the Illini Union on the Urbana campus of the University of
Illinois, April 26-29, 1964, ed. by Herbert Goldhor (Champaign: distributed
by the Illini Union Bookstore, ₍c1965₎), p.25-35.

[20] John R. Sharp, *Some Fundamentals of Information Retrieval* (New York
and London: House and Maxwell, 1965), p.83-86.

system having an average of 512 subject accesses will it be possible to evaluate such systems. Modern theory and reason are totally inadequate.

Not all information which the reference librarians of the future will produce will be retrieved. Some will be generated. Richard Hamming has published a proposal of a computer program which is a formula generator.[21] The user can instruct this program as to what he wishes to have a formula do, and the program will then generate the formula. Thereby, extensive searches of handbooks, searches which may or may not be successful, will be made unnecessary. Indeed, the program can generate programs which have not theretofore existed. This type of information generation will certainly be extended in the future. Other types of retrieval and generation will include Manfred Kochen's "encyclopedia."[22] Kochen looks forward to computer-produced bodies of information specifically designed for the use of one person—a technique which will surely be developed, albeit perhaps not in the next half-dozen years.

The most exciting implication for the future is the development of a new intellectual approach in librarianship. For most of the present century, scientists have looked upon nature as being a process instead of as a fixed and finished machine—the view held from the sixteenth through the nineteenth centuries. Similarly, historians since Voltaire and Turgot, in the middle of the eighteenth century, have written of man and his institutions as a process. But not all human institutions have been processes, or, at least, not all have had equal rates of change during the same periods of history. As the early part of this paper shows, libraries have been relatively static conceptually over a long period of time; libraries have experienced no major change since Dewey's introduction of the full-time reference assistant in 1884 and the advent of information centers in the 1920's, with the possible exception of the introduction of the photocopying machine for the patron's use. This is hardly a story of rapid evolution.

However, libraries now find themselves forced into a dynamic state of instability, which should not be confused with insecurity. Since the age of Pericles, the unstable periods in human history have been the most productive periods. Certainly, the period of instability into which libraries are now entering after a long period of changelessness will be one of the intellectually productive periods in librarianship.

---

[21] Richard W. Hamming, *Numerical Methods for Scientists and Engineers* (New York: McGraw-Hill, 1962), p.118-42.

[22] Manfred Kochen, *Some Problems in Information Science* (New York: Scarecrow Pr., 1965), p.156-59.

Systems thinking—with its new formulation of problems, its choice of more appropriate objectives, its hope for ingenuity in inventing new systems, and its recognition of the principle that library procedures are basically information processes—opens up whole new areas of thought about libraries. Perhaps the most important concomitant of systems thinking will be the increasing comprehensiveness of library systems, which alone stimulates a whole new intellectual approach to library problems. But perhaps of equal importance is the recognition of the principle that library procedures are information processes and not just techniques for moving physical objects from one place to another. However, were it not for the advent of the computer, it would not be possible to do much systems activation, for it is the computer which will enable librarians to manipulate information in library systems.

The computer, then, will radically change library procedures, particularly those involved in the production of the information store so necessary to reference librarians. In addition, the computer will facilitate the reference librarians' and the users' use of the information store. Associated with these two computer applications will be management information systems, which largely treat the computer as a source of information to be supplied to managers concerning both library and user processes. Finally, the computer will prove to be increasingly helpful in research work, for questions can now be asked for which it has hitherto been impossible to obtain answers. The computer's immense speed for manipulating data opens the way into large and hitherto inaccessible areas of the unknown.

So it is that systems thinking and computers are opening up entirely new areas in librarianship for intellectual pursuit. Certainly, implications for the future make the present a most exciting time to be a librarian.

Discussion

Darling: I have found this a highly stimulating three-day conference. As president-elect of the American Association of
School Librarians, I intend to go back to the Board and propose that we have a follow-up conference for school librarians, to explore further the implications for our type of
libraries of all we have heard.

Sattley: I want to ask a question, voice a dissent, and make a
statement. First, the question. Where are we today in relation to copyright and duplication of information? What is the
danger in this mass duplication?

Then the dissent and statement. Mr. Freiser is one of
the stimulating people in the profession, but he is not a person
to agree with completely, and I disagree with him often. The
other day he spoke of library education as an experience situation, and I feel this is not entirely in agreement with his library's practice of handing out predigested material to
students. As a practicing school librarian, I feel that we must
determine which students are ready for this kind of service;
we must think, also, of training the students who are going to
need to use college, university, and research libraries, and
we are training them. It is exciting to watch elementary-
school students in their first lessons on the encyclopedia or
the card catalog, for to them these are fun lessons. They are
stimulated to ask questions and to feel the excitement of
search and will, I am sure, become intelligent users of reference and research libraries.

Freiser: Nobody agrees more with Helen Sattley than I about providing educational experiences for students in the schools; nor
are we apart in our desire to give students the richest

experience and the best education. The details sometimes
differ, but this is where the fun is. By the way, we do not give
out predigested information. If anything, the schools up to
now, not because they wish to but because of technology and
because of the way they operate, have been dealing in digested
information—textbooks and a limited access to printed information through the abridged or the full *Readers' Guide*. This
is not predigested, but it is limited. Therefore, when we supply to students what amounts to a random access to the world's
literature, using as a start eighty indexes in the central library and relying on at least a twenty-million-volume group of
libraries, I would not say that we are handing out predigested
information.

As far as copyright is concerned, we are spending something like $40,000 or $50,000 a year to Xerox for our operation. We are not spending anything on fighting the copyright
fight at the present time. Everybody realizes this problem of
copyright, and we will come to some kind of conclusion. It
may be a royalty affair or what not. In the meantime the publishers, fortunately, are not going around smashing Xerox machines. Everybody knows there is a problem but everybody
knows also that all sides are trying to get together to find a
solution. In our particular shop, we continue to copy at a very
merry rate, with two 914's operating from 8:45 in the morning
until 9 o'clock at night. We have pointed out to the Canadian
publishers that, in the period of time since we started our
copying service, our book budget in the city schools has gone
from something like $80,000-$100,000 the first year we
started copying to $750,000 this year. Our periodical budgets
have multiplied by factors of five, ten, and fifteen. This, of
course, has been true in the States as well. May I have one
more minute to make a different comment?

Something has been left out of the discussions in the last
three days, namely, information. We keep talking about information retrieval, and it was mentioned by the last speaker
that text information is real information. This is what I find
hard to understand. Just as nature is not a machine so, as we
go back to the idea of Gutenberg, the printing press, the factory, and the printed page, information is not a printed paper;
or, to put it in another way, information is not a machine,
either. Again using this picture, we do not use a car as a
horse and carriage. The car did not change transportation;
the car changed housing; it changed our way of life, as far as
suburbs are concerned. In like manner, electronics is not
going to change bibliography. Electronics, it would seem to

me, is going to change our mode of communication. We will begin to understand in a new way what information is. It seems to me that information is real information in the sense of the event itself, the event we are reporting, the events we are comparing, the events we are even analyzing by comparing, the events which at the present time we have reports on. In discussing the user's needs, and this is all one concept here, we discuss the whole business of organizing information. Again, organizing seems to me a printed concept. We do not organize information; events organize information, or events give us information. In a sense, perhaps, I am asking our speaker a question: Is it possible that the new technology will give us some newer insights into what information may be, apart from printed reports, apart from bibliography, apart from organization? May we possibly come into contact with reality in a new way? I am not giving an answer here; I am suggesting a possible approach.

Kilgour: The answer to that was probably given in a paper that was published in 1948. This was a mathematical analysis which presented an atomistic idea of information. We can have a bit or no bit, but we cannot divide the bit; it is either one or nothing. This was a true atomistic idea which has been a very fruitful one in science for the past 150 years. The author of the 1948 paper, Claude Shannon, did what every great scientist does who has a great idea; he developed a concept of regularity throughout information, no matter what kind of information it was. And this regularity, of course, is what has made possible the remarkable developments in information processing and in information handling. Once again, this was done in the Bell Laboratories. They have done and will do an immense amount of work that has already led to and will continue to lead to a greater understanding of information.

CONFERENCE
ON THE PRESENT STATUS
AND FUTURE PROSPECTS
OF
REFERENCE / INFORMATION
SERVICE

March 30 – April 1, 1966

School of Library Service
Columbia University

Reference Services Division
American Library Association

Conference Director
Professor Winifred B. Linderman
School of Library Service
Columbia University

The Reference Services Division of the American Library Association and the School of Library Service of Columbia University have for some time been discussing independently the need for a new look at reference/ information service. This mutual interest, aided by a grant from the H. W. Wilson Foundation, has finally culminated in the present conference. The objectives have been stated for you and the speakers and participants have been selected in terms of these objectives.

The Conference has been planned as a working conference for persons actively interested in reference/information service in all its aspects as represented in various types of libraries and library education programs. Registrants have been invited in the full expectation that they will participate in the discussions of the conference.

PROGRAM

Wednesday, March 30

10 a.m.   Welcome and Introductions
        Jack Dalton, Dean
        Faculty of Library Service
        Columbia University

        Wayne M. Hartwell, President
        Reference Services Division
        American Library Association

        Keynote Address
        Verner W. Clapp, President
        Council on Library Resources, Inc.

2 p.m.   Consumers of Information and Levels of Service

        Users and Their Needs
        Helen M. Focke, Professor
        School of Library Science
        Western Reserve University

        The Spectrum of Services Offered
        Marian M. Allen, Assistant Librarian
          in charge of Reference Services
        University of Rochester Library

        Leonard H. Freiser, Chief Librarian
        Toronto Board of Education

        Alan M. Rees, Assistant Director for
          Research
        Center for Documentation and
          Communication Research
        School of Library Science
        Western Reserve University

        Moderator:
        Edward G. Strable, Executive Secretary
        ALA Reference Services Division

        Commentator:
        Frances E. Henne, Professor
        School of Library Service
        Columbia University

Thursday, March 31

10 a.m. Systems of Reference/Information Service

Regional and State
   John G. Lorenz, Deputy Librarian
     of Congress
   The Library of Congress

Subject Fields and National Networks
   Foster E. Mohrhardt, Director
   National Agricultural Library

Moderator:
   Richard J. Neuman, Librarian
   Salina Public Library

2 p.m. Reference/Information Sources

Survey of Currently Available Tools
   Katharine G. Harris, Reference Services
     Director
   Detroit Public Library

Development of Machine Generated Tools
   Pauline A. Atherton, Associate Director
   Documentation Research Project
   American Institute of Physics

Moderator:
   Oliver L. Lilley, Associate Professor
   School of Library Service
   Columbia University

Commentator:
   Edwin B. Colburn, Vice President
   and Chief of Indexing Services
   The H. W. Wilson Company

Friday, April 1

10 a.m. Information Storage and Retrieval Systems

Development of Storage and Retrieval Systems
   Joseph Becker, Data Processing Consultant
   Washington, D. C.

Intellectual Problems Involved
   Emmanuel G. Mesthene, Executive Director
   University Program on Technology and
     Society
   Harvard University

Moderator:
   Henry J. Dubester, Deputy Head
   Office of Science Information Service
   National Science Foundation

Commentator:
   Grieg Aspnes, Research Librarian
   Cargill, Incorporated

2:30
p.m. Implications for the Future
   Frederick G. Kilgour, Associate Librarian
   for Research and Development
   Yale University Library

Moderator:
   Phoebe F. Hayes, Director
   Bibliographical Center for Research
   Rocky Mountain Region, Inc.

4 p.m. Reception

Note: Discussion periods will follow the delivery of the
papers at each session.

Appendix II. *Registered Participants*

Scott Adams
Deputy Director
National Library of Medicine
Bethesda, Maryland

Marian M. Allen
Assistant Librarian, in charge of
   Reference Services
University of Rochester Library
Rochester, New York

Walter C. Allen
Head, Literature & Fine Arts
   Division
Dayton & Montgomery Co. Public
   Library
Dayton, Ohio

Grieg Aspnes
Research Librarian
Cargill, Incorporated
Minneapolis, Minnesota

Effie C. Astbury
Associate Professor
Graduate School of Library Science
McGill University
Montreal, Canada

Mrs. Pauline Atherton
Associate Director
Documentation Research Project
American Institute of Physics
New York, New York

Jo Ann Aufdenkamp
Librarian
Federal Reserve Bank of Chicago
Chicago, Illinois

Mrs. Julia Bartling
Head, Reference Department
University of Iowa Library
Iowa City, Iowa

Joseph Becker
Data Processing Consultant
Bethesda, Maryland

Florence Blakely
Head, Reference Department
Duke University Library
Durham, North Carolina

Martha Boaz
Dean, School of Library Science
University of Southern California
Los Angeles, California

Agnes Brite
Librarian
New England Mutual Life
   Insurance Co.
Boston, Massachusetts

John S. Burgan
Head, County Services
Enoch Pratt Free Library
Baltimore, Maryland

190

Charles H. Busha
Reference Consultant
South Carolina State Library Board
Columbia, South Carolina

Kirk Cabeen
Assistant Director
Engineering Societies Library
New York, New York

Leon Carnovsky
Professor of Library Science
Graduate Library School
University of Chicago
Chicago, Illinois

James Chandler
Chief Reference Librarian
C.I.A. Library
Washington, D.C.

Mrs. Frances Neel Cheney
Associate Director and
    Associate Professor
Peabody Library School
George Peabody College
Nashville, Tennessee

Antoinette Ciolli
Chief Science Librarian
Brooklyn College Library
Brooklyn, New York

Verner W. Clapp
President
Council on Library Resources, Inc.
Washington, D.C.

Virginia Clark
Reference Librarian
Kenyon College
Gambier, Ohio

Jack A. Clarke
Assistant Director and
    Associate Professor
Library School
University of Wisconsin
Madison, Wisconsin

Marguerite V. Clayton
Assistant Professor

School of Library Science
Texas Woman's University
Denton, Texas

Virginia L. Close
Head, Department of Reference
    Services and Assistant Librarian
Dartmouth College Libraries
Hanover, New Hampshire

Edwin B. Colburn
Vice-President and Chief of
    Indexing Services
The H.W. Wilson Company
Bronx, New York

Catherine M. Corgan
Assistant Librarian and Head of
    Adult Services
Osterhout Free Library
Wilkes-Barre, Pennsylvania

Jean E. Crabtree
Head Librarian
Garden City Senior High School
Garden City, New York

Jack Dalton
Dean
Faculty of Library Service
Columbia University
New York, New York

Richard L. Darling
Assistant Director
Department of Instructional
    Materials
Montgomery County Public Schools
Rockville, Maryland

Henry J. Dubester
Deputy Head
Office of Science Information Service
National Science Foundation
Washington, D.C.

Shirley H. Edsall
Librarian
The Arthur A. Houghton, Jr.
    Library
Corning Community College
Corning, New York

John Fall
Chief of the Economics Division
New York Public Library
New York, New York

Helen M. Focke
Professor
School of Library Science
Western Reserve University
Cleveland, Ohio

Ruth R. Frame
Director, Professional Services
Michigan State Library
Lansing, Michigan

Leonard H. Freiser
Chief Librarian
Toronto Board of Education
Toronto, Canada

Thomas J. Galvin
Director of Students and
   Assistant Professor
School of Library Science
Simmons College
Boston, Massachusetts

Robert G. Gaylor
Director of Readers Services
Kresge Library
Oakland University
Rochester, Michigan

Theodore F. Gould
Assistant Librarian for
   Public Services
University of California, Davis
Davis, California

Mrs. Margaret Hayes Grazier
Associate Professor
Library Science Department
Wayne State University
Detroit, Michigan

Roger C. Greer
Director of Libraries
State University College
Potsdam, New York

Laurel Grotzinger
Assistant Professor

Department of Librarianship
Western Michigan University
Kalamazoo, Michigan

Robert D. Harlan
Assistant Professor
School of Librarianship
University of California
Berkeley, California

Katharine G. Harris
Reference Services Director
Detroit Public Library
Detroit, Michigan

Wayne M. Hartwell
President, ALA Reference
   Services Division
Librarian, Editorial Department
F. E. Compton Company
Chicago, Illinois

Henry C. Hastings
Head, Reference Department
Gary Public Library
Gary, Indiana

Phoebe F. Hayes
Director
Bibliographical Center for Research
Rocky Mountain Region, Inc.
Denver, Colorado

Frances E. Henne
Professor of Library Service
School of Library Service
Columbia University
New York, New York

James J. Heslin
Director
The New York Historical Society
New York, New York

Mrs. Marjorie Holt
Director of Reference and Research
Brooklyn Public Library
Brooklyn, New York

Norman Horrocks
Librarian
West Australian Institute of Technology
Perth, Australia

Mrs. Dorothy Truesdale Humes
Consultant, Information Services
Rochester Public Library
Rochester, New York

Mrs. Frances B. Jenkins
Professor
Graduate School of Library Science
University of Illinois
Urbana, Illinois

Marion E. Kanaly
Associate Librarian for Readers'
   Services
Wellesley College Library
Wellesley, Massachusetts

William A. Katz
Associate Professor
Department of Library Science
University of Kentucky
Lexington, Kentucky

Margaret Keefe
Head, Business and Industry
   Department
Flint Public Library
Flint, Michigan

Frederick G. Kilgour
Associate Librarian for Research
   and Development
Yale University Library
New Haven, Connecticut

Katharine L. Kinder
Chief Librarian
Johns-Manville Research and
   Engineering Center
Manville, New Jersey

Joseph Klimberger
Reference Coordinator
Nassau Library System
Hempstead, New York

Mrs. Judith F. Krug
Research Analyst
Office for Research and
   Development
American Library Association
Chicago, Illinois

Robert G. Krupp
Chief, Science and Technology
   Division
New York Public Library
New York, New York

Ivan Kvakovszky
Assistant Professor
Department of Library Science
Kent State University
Kent, Ohio

Robert H. Land
Chief, General Reference and
   Bibliography Division
The Library of Congress
Washington, D.C.

Oliver L. Lilley
Associate Professor of Library
   Service
Columbia University
New York, New York

Winifred B. Linderman
Professor of Library Service
School of Library Service
Columbia University
New York, New York

Ardis Lodge
Head, Reference Department
University Research Library
University of California, L.A.
Los Angeles, California

John G. Lorenz
Deputy Librarian of Congress
The Library of Congress
Washington, D.C.

Haynes McMullen
Professor of Library Science
Division of Library Science
Indiana University
Bloomington, Indiana

Emmanuel G. Mesthene
Executive Director
Program on Technology and Society
Harvard University
Cambridge, Massachusetts

Robert A. Miller
Assistant Professor of Library
  Science
University of North Carolina
Chapel Hill, North Carolina

Foster E. Mohrhardt
Director
National Agricultural Library
Washington, D.C.

Perry D. Morrison
Associate Professor of
  Librarianship
School of Librarianship
University of Washington
Seattle, Washington

William D. Murphy
Librarian
Kirkland, Ellis, Hodson, Chaffetz
  and Masters
Chicago, Illinois

Florence B. Murray
Professor of Library Science
School of Library Science
University of Toronto
Toronto, Canada

Richard J. Neuman
Librarian
Salina Public Library
Salina, Kansas

Natalie N. Nicholson
Associate Director, Reader Services
Massachusetts Institute of
  Technology Libraries
Cambridge, Massachusetts

Mrs. Elizabeth W. Owens
Chief Librarian
Union Electric Company
St. Louis, Missouri

Agnes L. Reagan
Associate Professor of
  Librarianship
Division of Librarianship
Emory University
Atlanta, Georgia

Mrs. Patricia Reeling
Assistant to the Conference Director
Clifton, New Jersey

Alan M. Rees
Assistant Director for Research
Center for Documentation and
  Communication Research
Western Reserve University
Cleveland, Ohio

Harry B. Reiff
Head, Social Sciences and
  Technology Department
Northeast Regional Library
Free Library of Philadelphia
Philadelphia, Pennsylvania

Michael M. Reynolds
Assistant Director of Libraries
Indiana University
Bloomington, Indiana

Giles Robertson
Head of Public Services
University of Illinois,
  Chicago Circle
Chicago, Illinois

Elizabeth Rumics
Head, Readers Services
Oberlin College Library
Oberlin, Ohio

Louis D. Sass
Dean
Graduate Library School
Pratt Institute
Brooklyn, New York

Helen R. Sattley
Director, School Library Service
New York City Board of Education
New York, New York

Lewis J. Scher
Librarian
Jamaica High School
Jamaica, New York

Julia Schwartz
Assistant Reference Librarian
University of South Florida Library
Tampa, Florida

Thomas S. Shaw
Professor
Library School
Louisiana State University
Baton Rouge, Louisiana

Eugene P. Sheehy
Head, Reference Department
Columbia University Libraries
New York, New York

Martha Shepard
Chief of the Reference Division
National Library of Canada
Ottawa, Canada

Richard Shoemaker
Professor of Library Service
Graduate School of Library Service
Rutgers University
New Brunswick, New Jersey

Thomas P. Slavens
Instructor in Library Science
Department of Library Science
University of Michigan
Ann Arbor, Michigan

Norman D. Stevens
Associate Librarian
Rutgers University Library
New Brunswick, New Jersey

Edward G. Strable
Executive Secretary
Reference Services Division
American Library Association
Chicago, Illinois

Peggy Sullivan
Director
Knapp School Libraries Project
American Library Association
Chicago, Illinois

Robert M. Thomas
Assistant Coordinator, Adult Services
New York Public Library
New York, New York

Lola Rivers Thompson
Assistant Professor
Graduate School of Library Science
University of Texas
Austin, Texas

Mrs. Irma R. Tomberlin
Assistant Professor
School of Library Science
University of Oklahoma
Norman, Oklahoma

David Turiel
Adult Services Consultant
Westchester Library System
Mount Vernon, New York

Bernard Vavrek
Teaching Fellow in Library Science
Graduate School of Library and
    Information Sciences
University of Pittsburgh
Pittsburgh, Pennsylvania

Mathilde Verner
Assistant Professor
Department of Library Science
Catholic University of America
Washington, D.C.

John N. Waddell
Senior Lecturer in Library Service
School of Library Service
Columbia University
New York, New York

David R. Watkins
Head of Reference
Yale University Library
New Haven, Connecticut

Henry Wieman
Assistant Librarian
Oak Park and River Forest High
    School
Oak Park, Illinois

Mrs. Joan Wilts
Assistant Professor of Library
    Science
Rosary College
River Forest, Illinois

Bohdan S. Wynar
Associate Professor
Graduate School of Librarianship
University of Denver
Denver, Colorado